Developing Middleware in Java EE 8

Build robust middleware solutions using the latest
technologies and trends

Abdalla Mahmoud

BIRMINGHAM - MUMBAI

Developing Middleware in Java EE 8

Commissioning Editor: Aaron Lazar
Acquisition Editor: Sandeep Mishra
Content Development Editor: Akshada Iyer
Technical Editor: Mehul Singh
Copy Editor: Safis Editing
Project Coordinator: Prajakta Naik
Proofreader: Safis Editing
Indexer: Tejal Daruwale Soni
Graphics: Jisha Chirayil
Production Coordinator: Aparna Bhagat

First published: June 2018

Production reference: 1290618

Published by Packt Publishing Ltd.
Livery Place
35 Livery Street
Birmingham
B3 2PB, UK.

ISBN 978-1-78839-107-8

www.packtpub.com

To my mother, RIP, for growing me up and making me who I'm,
To my father, for every moment he encouraged me to make my dreams come true,
To my loving wife, for the continuous love and support she gives me,
To my lovely daughter, for setting a meaning to my life,
To Akshada Iyer, for all the efforts she exerted to get this book done,
And, to the Packt editorial team, for all the support they gave me.

`mapt.io`

Mapt is an online digital library that gives you full access to over 5,000 books and videos, as well as industry leading tools to help you plan your personal development and advance your career. For more information, please visit our website.

Why subscribe?

- Spend less time learning and more time coding with practical eBooks and Videos from over 4,000 industry professionals

- Improve your learning with Skill Plans built especially for you

- Get a free eBook or video every month

- Mapt is fully searchable

- Copy and paste, print, and bookmark content

PacktPub.com

Did you know that Packt offers eBook versions of every book published, with PDF and ePub files available? You can upgrade to the eBook version at `www.PacktPub.com` and as a print book customer, you are entitled to a discount on the eBook copy. Get in touch with us at `service@packtpub.com` for more details.

At `www.PacktPub.com`, you can also read a collection of free technical articles, sign up for a range of free newsletters, and receive exclusive discounts and offers on Packt books and eBooks.

Contributors

About the author

Abdalla Mahmoud is a Java software architect and trainer with 14+ years of experience in the software development industry. He's led many successful projects using a broad range of technologies and frameworks covering the most out of the web, desktop, and mobile development aspects. He's also contributed in training hundreds of Java software engineers for more than 7 years, on different topics including Java EE, Spring, design patterns, and Android.

About the reviewer

Borja Pérez Dopazo is a software engineer who lives in Negreira, Spain. He works as a software architect and product developer for SMTecnología. His projects include the co-creation of Trebolet, a smart forms generation system in Java and Angular, with which he aims to conquer the business world. Passionate about traveling, racket sports, and food (not necessarily in that order), he tries to make a name for himself in the world from his small town in the beautiful area of Galicia.

I want to thank my parents for helping me strive to be better.

Packt is searching for authors like you

If you're interested in becoming an author for Packt, please visit `authors.packtpub.com` and apply today. We have worked with thousands of developers and tech professionals, just like you, to help them share their insight with the global tech community. You can make a general application, apply for a specific hot topic that we are recruiting an author for, or submit your own idea.

Table of Contents

Preface

This book is all about learning Java features, such as JAX-RS, EJBs, and JPAs, and also about building powerful middleware for newer architectures, such as the cloud. We will also be designing and implementing professional enterprise middleware solutions using the latest techniques and features provided by the Java EE 8 platform.

Who this book is for

Enterprise architects, designers, developers, and programmers who are interested in learning how to build robust middleware solutions for enterprise software will find this book useful. Prior knowledge of Java EE is essential.

What this book covers

Chapter 1, *Delving into Java EE 8*, explores the Java EE 88 APIs and the awesome new features added since the previous version. Moreover, it shows you what software and tools we will use throughout the chapters of this book, and how to download, install, and use them.

Chapter 2, *Dependency Injection Using CDI 2.0*, teaches you about the dependency management problem and how the CDI API provides a complete and easy-to-use framework to manage your enterprise-level dependencies.

Chapter 3, *Accessing the Database with JPA 2.1*, allows you to manipulate the most important part of enterprise applications—the database. The Java Persistence API provides a mature solution for accessing your data, eliminating the gap between your relational database model and application object-oriented models by implementing the object-to-relational mappings technique.

Chapter 4, *Validating Data with Bean Validation 2.0*, explores how to handle a common and important aspect of your enterprise application, data validation. With the bean validation API, you will be able to add all your validation rules using declarative methods, and without any verbose coding.

Chapter 5, *Exposing Web Services with JAX-RS 2.1*, assists you in learning about the most important API to go with your application into the cloud, JAX-RS. With JAX-RS, you will expose your business functions as RESTful services to be consumed by other applications in the cloud, including your application itself.

Chapter 6, *Manipulating JSON with JSON-B 1.0*, demonstrates how to serialize/deserialize JSON data, and how to customize the format and the output for your returned JSON from RESTful services.

Chapter 7, *Communicating with Different Systems with JMS 2.0*, outlines the difference between point-to-point (p2p) and publish-subscribe model architectures, and how you can implement both of them using JMS. You will learn how to write message-driven beans to handle messages, and you will also learn how to use programmatic communication with JMS to obtain new messages from external systems.

Chapter 8, *Sending Mails with JavaMail 1.6*, showcases the method to send mails from inside your middleware solution to your end users, using the JavaMail API. You will learn how to provide configuration for your SMTP server, how to include HTML in your mail, and how to include inline images inside.

Chapter 9, *Securing an Application with Java Security 1.0*, familiarizes you with providing user credentials and authorities from the database and how to use the different authentication mechanisms provided by the API. In addition, you will learn how to implement an OAuth system in your web services, similar to the ones used by popular services like Facebook and GitHub, providing a widely used standard for obtaining access credentials to your system. With OAuth, you can later extend your authentication mechanism to log in using external, systems such as Facebook and GitHub.

Chapter 10, *Making Interactive Applications with WebSockets 1.1*, presents the Web Sockets technology, how it works, and how it's used to build user-interactive real-time applications. You will learn how to build WebSockets endpoints using WebSockets 1.1 API, how to handle a live connection lifecycle method, and how to maintain client state.

Chapter 11, *Writing Business Logic with EJB 3.2*, explains the concept of Enterprise JavaBeans, why you should wrap your business logic inside them, and what services it provides to code. You learn about the different types of Enterprise JavaBeans and in which contexts you should use each one of them.

To get the most out of this book

1. Readers are expected to have basic knowledge of Java and Java EE
2. They need to install Eclipse or NetBeans with GlassFish server before they can actually begin

Download the example code files

You can download the example code files for this book from your account at www.packtpub.com. If you purchased this book elsewhere, you can visit www.packtpub.com/support and register to have the files emailed directly to you.

You can download the code files by following these steps:

1. Log in or register at www.packtpub.com.
2. Select the **SUPPORT** tab.
3. Click on **Code Downloads & Errata**.
4. Enter the name of the book in the **Search** box and follow the onscreen instructions.

Once the file is downloaded, please make sure that you unzip or extract the folder using the latest version of:

- WinRAR/7-Zip for Windows
- Zipeg/iZip/UnRarX for Mac
- 7-Zip/PeaZip for Linux

The code bundle for the book is also hosted on GitHub at https://github.com/PacktPublishing/Developing-Middleware-in-Java-EE-8. In case there's an update to the code, it will be updated on the existing GitHub repository.

We also have other code bundles from our rich catalog of books and videos available at https://github.com/PacktPublishing/. Check them out!

Download the color images

We also provide a PDF file that has color images of the screenshots/diagrams used in this book. You can download it here: https://www.packtpub.com/sites/default/files/downloads/DevelopingMiddlewareinJavaEE8_ColorImages.pdf.

Conventions used

There are a number of text conventions used throughout this book.

CodeInText: Indicates code words in text, database table names, folder names, filenames, file extensions, pathnames, dummy URLs, user input, and Twitter handles. Here is an example: "The interface includes one abstract method—onMessage(Message msg)."

A block of code is set as follows:

```
public class ClientMDB implements MessageListener {

    @Override
    public void onMessage(Message msg) {
        // cast message and process it here
    }

}
```

When we wish to draw your attention to a particular part of a code block, the relevant lines or items are set in bold:

```
@Inject
@JMSConnectionFactory("java:app/jms/MyConnectionFactory")
private JMSContext context;
```

Any command-line input or output is written as follows:

```
******** Hello JMS!
```

Bold: Indicates a new term, an important word, or words that you see onscreen. For example, words in menus or dialog boxes appear in the text like this. Here is an example: "From the **Common Tasks** pane, navigate to **Resources** | **JMS Resources** | **Destination Resources**"

 Warnings or important notes appear like this.

 Tips and tricks appear like this.

Get in touch

Feedback from our readers is always welcome.

General feedback: Email feedback@packtpub.com and mention the book title in the subject of your message. If you have questions about any aspect of this book, please email us at questions@packtpub.com.

Errata: Although we have taken every care to ensure the accuracy of our content, mistakes do happen. If you have found a mistake in this book, we would be grateful if you would report this to us. Please visit www.packtpub.com/submit-errata, selecting your book, clicking on the Errata Submission Form link, and entering the details.

Piracy: If you come across any illegal copies of our works in any form on the Internet, we would be grateful if you would provide us with the location address or website name. Please contact us at copyright@packtpub.com with a link to the material.

If you are interested in becoming an author: If there is a topic that you have expertise in and you are interested in either writing or contributing to a book, please visit authors.packtpub.com.

Reviews

Please leave a review. Once you have read and used this book, why not leave a review on the site that you purchased it from? Potential readers can then see and use your unbiased opinion to make purchase decisions, we at Packt can understand what you think about our products, and our authors can see your feedback on their book. Thank you!

For more information about Packt, please visit packtpub.com.

Delving into Java EE 8 1

Welcome to our developing middleware solutions using Java EE 8 journey. In this book, we'll study and practice how to perfectly design and implement middleware solutions using the Java EE 8 APIs.

Whether you're a newbie or an existing user of Java EE, we've tried to make this book useful to you. For those who are new to Java EE, at the beginning of each chapter, we introduce the essential technical concepts that will enable you to move on your way. Also, for those who are already using Java EE, we've provided separate chapters for the new APIs that were introduced in release 8, in addition to mentioning in each chapter what new features were introduced for those existing APIs.

In this chapter, we will look into the following topics:

- What is Java EE?
- Chapter roadmap
- Required software
- Book project

What is Java EE?

Java EE is a very popular platform for building enterprise solutions in the Java programming language. For many years, it has reached the top of the list of the most important enterprise application development platforms, with success in nearly all aspects of enterprise application development.

Java EE provides application developers with the following:

- **Application Server**: A fully-featured middleware with all of the functionalities required to build enterprise applications
- **Java EE APIs**: A set of APIs covering the common functionalities required by application developers to implement their enterprise solutions

Our role, as application developers and architects, is to design our solution as a set of components. Those components will use the Java EE APIs.

Enterprise applications

For me, enterprise applications was always a buzzy term. If we substituted enterprise with the word business, it would become business applications, which is, in fact, misleading and a far cry from the true meaning of the term.

The term *enterprise applications* refer to the type of applications that are used by a group of users. These types of applications include nearly everything around us—social networks, business applications, productivity applications, gaming, chatting, and so on. If we conduct a simple analysis of the commonalities between all of them, we will find that some of their common characteristics include:

- The applications are used by a group of users, with different levels of authority over the provided functionalities
- The applications require special scaling and resource management techniques to be applied in order to be able to handle heavy loads when the application gets more active users or more data
- The application should run on a robust environment, robust enough to provide near 100% system availability
- The applications manage an operational database, with hundreds or thousands of operations performed each second, while keeping our data consistent and responsive

Java EE is you a platform that fulfills all of the aforementioned requirements, and more, with declarative and easy-to-use methodologies. Rather than investing time and effort into those non-functional requirements, you'll build your applications above a middleware software, providing you with a ready-to-use implementation for all required services, leaving you free to focus on your business logic.

Java EE architecture

The Java EE platform follows the four-tier architecture, the tiers being as follows:

- **EIS tier:** This is the **enterprise information system (EIS)** tier, where we store and retrieve all of our business data. Usually, it's a relational database system that's accessed using the Java Persistence API through our business tier, as will be discussed in detail in this book.

- **Business tier:** The business tier is responsible for managing business components that expose functionalities to other modules or separate systems. Enterprise JavaBeans, messaging, and other services are maintained in this tier, which will be discussed in detail in this book.

- **Web tier:** The web tier is where your web components/pages live. Although the Java's EE web profile is out of the scope of this book, we've used the web tier in many examples as well as in this chapter; therefore, basic knowledge about Servlets and JSP is essential.

- **Client tier:** Either a thin client (web browser) or a thick one (another Java application) that consumes the services we provide in our enterprise middleware solution.

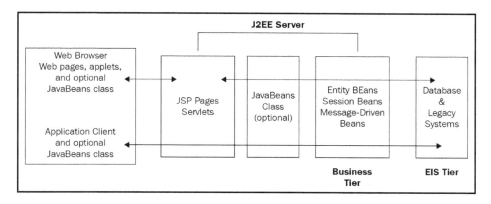

Note that, in this book, we'll be focusing more on the EIS and business tier parts of an enterprise middleware solution, the web part being out of the scope of this book.

Chapter roadmap

The learning journey we'll be moving on alongside the next chapter is planned to be as follows:

- We'll start by introducing the concept of dependency injection and how to use it to simplify management processes, and the different dependencies and resources your application maintains.
- We'll move on to data management topics by learning how to map your data into relational databases using the Java Persistence API, and how to validate your business objects against your business rules using the Java Validation API.
- Next, we'll learn how to encapsulate business logic and expose it to other layers by learning how to build business components using the Enterprise JavaBeans API, and how to expose your business functionalities into RESTful services using the Java API for RESTful services, JAX-RS. We'll also cover a newly introduced API, JSON-B 1.0, and learn how to use it to perform complex JSON processing operations.
- After that, we'll learn about another system-to-system communication model, which is messaging. We'll understand the concepts and architectural philosophy of messaging techniques, and learn how to apply our knowledge using JMS 2.0.
- Then, we'll learn how to send notifications to our system users and send other information by sending them emails using the JavaMail API.
- Then, we'll learn how to build interactive web applications with real-time communication using the WebSockets API.
- Then, we'll learn how to secure our enterprise applications using the newly introduced Java Security API, and how to provide authentication and authorization features for any enterprise application, with this easy-to-use API.

Here's a full list of the main APIs we'll be covering in this book:

- **Contexts and Dependency Injection (CDI)** 2.0
- Java Persistence API 2.1
- Bean Validation API 2.0
- Enterprise JavaBeans 3.2
- Java API for RESTful Services JAX-RS 2.1
- **JSON-Binding (JSON-B)** API 1.0 (new)
- **Java Messaging System (JMS)** 2.0

- JavaMail 1.6.
- Java Security 1.0 (new)
- WebSockets 1.1

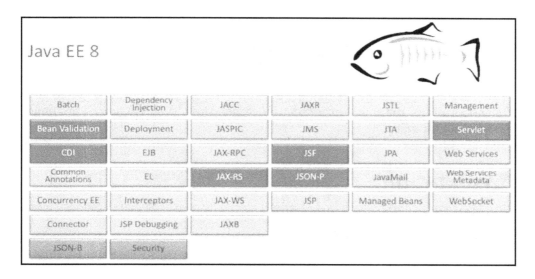

Contexts and dependency injection

When designing an enterprise solution, one of the primary tasks is to divide your application into separate components that interact with each other. To avoid all the hassle of managing our components, their dependencies, and their life cycles, the **contexts and dependency API (CDI)** has been developed to be the backbone of component and dependency management. By components, we mean objects that encapsulate your application's business logic. By dependencies, we mean commonly used application-shared resources such as a database connection, user sessions, web service endpoints, and such.

In Chapter 2, *Dependency Injection Using CDI 2.0*, we'll learn how to create and use CDI beans, how to use bean scopes, how to provide different implementations of the same bean, and how to inject beans into other beans. Moreover, we'll learn about some more advanced topics, such as producers, interceptors, and events.

Data persistence

The data access layer is the most fundamental part of any enterprise application. A common problem arises when dealing with a relational database from an object-oriented system—all runtime data are represented as objects, where the real data is stored as rows in tables. The **Java Persistence API (JPA)** provides Java developers with all the required operations, mappings, and techniques for mapping objects to the relational database.

In Chapter 3, *Accessing the Database with JPA 2.1*, we'll learn how to create and use JPA entities and map them to tables and columns. Moreover, we'll learn how to perform the four CRUD operations: mapping entity relationships, using the JPA Query Language and the Criteria API, and mapping inheritance relationships.

Data validation

Validating your application's data is a required step before any of your business operations. Jakarta EE provides the Java Validation API, which integrates well with other APIs, like JPA and JAX-RS. With this API, you can declare all your validation rules to be processed automatically for you, whenever you receive new data from the user. It's as easy as annotating your domain objects with the appropriate annotation.

In Chapter 4, *Validating Data with Bean Validation 2.0*, we'll learn how to use the Java Validation API to perform programmatic and automatic bean validation, how to validate graphs of objects in a bean, and the different validation constraints available. Moreover, we'll learn how to validate bean method parameters and return values, and how to define custom validation constraints to handle more complex and recurrent validation scenarios.

Enterprise JavaBeans

The core composing components of an enterprise application in Jakarta EE are Enterprise JavaBeans. They are plain Java objects with embedded business logic, supported by different services from the business tier, such as remoting, transaction management, user session management, timer services, and more.

In this book, we'll learn what enterprise Java beans are, what are they used for, and what services they provide for your embedded business code. We'll study and practice the three available types of sessions bean: stateless, stateful, and singleton.

RESTful services

RESTful services are a key technology for making computer systems talk to each other and, more specifically, making application frontends talk to their backends, and sometimes to other third-party integrations. They are functions that are deployed on a server and can be called remotely from any other system. RESTful is not just another protocol for remoting with HTTP; it's a full architectural style used to build your enterprise applications and make them extensible by other modules or separate systems.

In Chapter 5, *Exposing Web Services with JAX-RS 2.1*, we will learn what RESTful services are and how to create your own RESTful services using JAX-RS. Moreover, we'll learn how to use Postman to test your RESTful services. JAX-RS topics such as accepting and processing user parameters, producing JSON responses, and uploading files are all covered in this chapter. In the final section, we'll learn about the newly introduced support for server-sent events in JAX-RS and look at examples of how to use it to provide your clients with on-demand real-time notifications about different business events.

JSON processing

As JSON is a very common format for exchanging data in REST operations, the need for a native API in Java to perform advanced processing over JSON has arisen. Finally, Jakarta EE was introduced?

In this book, we'll get an introduction to the newly introduced API, the JSON Binding API, and see how we can use it to directly manipulate JSON in advanced contexts with practical examples.

Messaging

Software-to-software messaging is another model of how software communicates with each other. In this model, a messaging middleware stands in the middle of a sender and a receiver to enable the reliable exchange of messages even if one of the two parties is out of service. Moreover, this model enables the application of scaling techniques such as load balancing and message broadcasting to subscribed components.

In this book, we'll learn the basic principles of messaging and how the JMS API provides a comprehensive framework to build a full-featured messaging system to realize the described messaging model. We'll also learn the difference between the two messaging models—**Point-to-Point (P2P)** and the Publish-Subscribe model—and how to implement both of them, with examples, using the JMS API.

Mailing

Software-to-user communication is also essential in any enterprise application. Software needs to mail its users about notifications, updates, changes, password change confirmations, and so on. Although in a large-scale development, a separate third-party cloud mailing solution would be a good idea, it's still very common to directly use the mailing APIs to communicate with our users, especially in small-scale developments.

In Chapter 8, *Sending Mails with JavaMail 1.6*, we'll get a brief introduction to the main mailing protocols. After that, we'll learn and practice how to programmatically send plain text and HTML emails, in addition to optionally attaching files to your emails.

WebSockets

WebSockets is one of the major overall advancements in HTTP communication. It extends HTTP to allow it to handle one or more full-duplex communication channels over a single HTTP connection, enabling all kinds of applications with real-time communication requirements to appear on the web market, such as chatting, multi-player gaming, collaborative document editing, and many more.

In Chapter 8, *Sending Mails with JavaMail 1.6*, we'll learn what WebSockets are and when to use them. Moreover, we'll learn and practice how to create WebSockets endpoints in Java and how to create a client for them in JavaScript. In addition, we'll learn how to maintain and encode user state in our server. At the end of the chapter, we'll look at a complete example of using WebSockets to implement a cinema tickets booking interface for our book's project.

Security

Authentication and authorization are the most important aspects of any middleware solution. Any enterprise application should provide a way to authenticate users before letting them in and should also check their authorization before availing any functionality to them.

Although JACC and JASPIC have existed since the early days of Java EE, they have gotten more complicated as a result of their continuous evolution. The need to restructure the Security API was a priority request by Java EE developers over the years and, therefore, the Java Security API 1.0 was introduced in Jakarta EE 8.

In Chapter 9, *Securing an Application with Java Security 1.0*, we'll learn the concepts and terminology related to this new API and how to get started with it by creating a simple login example. Moreover, we'll take a more in-depth look at basic concepts, such as identity stores, authentication context objects, and authentication mechanisms.

Required software

You'll need to install the following software in order to be able to follow and run through the examples in each chapter:

IDE

Whatever your preferred IDE is—Eclipse, NetBeans, IntelliJ, Notepad, or Nano—you'll be able to use, modify, and run this book's examples. If you're confused, I recommend using NetBeans, as it's the community's fully-featured one, with the least configuration needed to get started with our book. Keep in mind that full support for Jakarta EE 8 may not be available yet for those IDEs when you read this book. However, all you need to do is to configure your application's server path to a GlassFish 5 edition. Even if your IDE cannot recognize Glassfish Version 5 yet, there are workarounds available to make it appear like version 4; you can Google it if you cannot configure Glassfish 5 with your favorite IDE.

Application server

Any application server can be used as long, as it fully implements the Jakarta EE 8 profile. At the time of writing, only the reference implementation (Glassfish 5) was available with full support for version 8. Therefore, all examples in this book have been written and tested on Glassfish 5 therefore, I recommend using it, as all the related instructions and configurations are written for this application server specifically and other application servers may require additional configurations that you may have to perform on your own.

Build tool

Either Maven or Gradle would help; however, we've used Maven 3 for the examples in this book.

Relational database system

Any relational database would also be suitable. We've selected MySQL for the database examples in this book, as it's one of the most popular open source databases widely used in thousands of successful data-intensive applications.

However, if you prefer to use your own database server, you can, as long as it's JDBC compliant. However, in that case, you'll have to figure the own configurations required for the examples yourself, as we've used MySQL as the default database server for all the examples in this book.

Book project

Throughout the chapters of this book, we'll be working on an imaginary real-world project to apply the examples too. The project is simple and interesting; it's a cinema ticket booking application. Although we mention this application in the coming chapters, we don't have its complete final version! We're just using some of its requirements to learn about the different APIs and features in Jakarta EE.

Our application should have the following features:

- CRUD movies, cinemas, and seats
- Allow users to browse movies, cinemas, and seats
- Allow users to browse seats for a cinema on a specific date and pick one or more tickets

Our master scene for our booking application is the interactive booking board, as shown in the following screenshot:

Book a Seat											
Seats for Movie with ID 27											
001	002	003	004	005	006	007	008	009	010	011	012
013	014	015	016	017	018	019	020	021	022	023	024
025	026	027	028	029	030	031	032	033	034	035	036
037	038	039	040	041	042	043	044	045	046	047	048
049	050	051	052	053	054	055	056	057	058	059	060
061	062	063	064	065	066	067	068	069	070	071	072
073	074	075	076	077	078	079	080	081	082	083	084
085	086	087	088	089	090	091	092	093	094	095	096
097	098	099	100	101	102	103	104	105	106	107	108
109	110	111	112	113	114	115	116	117	118	119	120
121	122	123	124	125	126	127	128	129	130	131	132
133	134	135	136	137	138	139	140	141	142	143	144
145	146	147	148	149	150	151	152	153	154	155	156
157	158	159	160	161	162	163	164	165	166	167	168

This interactive board will be our last practical example in this book, before we end by securing our applications in the last chapter.

Goodbye Java EE, welcome Jakarta EE!

What's the story behind this new name that suddenly appeared on the market, Jakarta EE? Well, for many years, Java EE was one of the top choices when talking about enterprise application development. Over the years, thousands of mission-critical applications have been developed using Java EE, proving that this technology is robust enough to be power the infrastructure of the biggest enterprises on the globe.

However, with the rapid advances in technology, more frequent releases, covering all the new requirements needed in a dynamic, changing world, have always been the top request of the thousands of developers using it, and things started to get a bit late to the market, compared to other quickly evolving technologies, such as Spring.

Therefore, the Java Community Process has decided to pass the management of Java EE to the Eclipse Foundation, where it will keep evolving, but under the new brand name, Jakarta EE.

According to their announcement, the Jakarta EE working group aims to:

- Deliver more frequent releases
- Reduce barriers to participation
- Develop the community
- Manage the Jakarta EE brand on behalf of the community

Summary

Now, having introduced the topic we'll be covering in this book and taken a quick look at the roadmap of the learning plan we'll go with, let's get ready and start our journey by moving on to `Chapter 2`, *Dependency Injection Using CDI 2.0*. Ensure that you have installed all of the required software, and then, let's move on!

Dependency Injection Using CDI 2.0

CDI (**Contexts and Dependency Injection**) is one of the most essential and powerful APIs in Java EE. With CDI, you can easily divide your application into separate components interacting with each other, avoiding all the hassles of managing your components, life cycles, calling JNDI, and any other redundant programmatic work. Although the initial goal of CDI was to provide an easy mechanism for tying the web layer to the data access layer, CDI now has a broader scope of usage and implementation scenarios. Let's take an overview of the key features that CDI provides to our middleware solution:

- **DI (Dependency Injection)**: A popular technique for supplying components with other components they depend on. CDI provides a declarative approach for defining components and their scope of life, and of course obtaining them back. Moreover, DI in Java EE is used to easily retrieve essential platform components such as data sources, entity managers, enterprise Java beans, messaging destinations, and more.
- **Interceptors**: Interceptors provide a simple mechanism for handling cross-cutting concerns in enterprise applications. Interceptors are methods that can be forced to precede the call to a set of other methods, in order to perform pre and/or post operations that are common among them, such as logging, transaction management, and more. This technique is commonly referred to by the term *aspect-oriented programming*.
- **Event Handling**: Events are incidents that occur in our application, where one or more different objects are interested to react to. CDI provides a model for publishing events, where other objects can subscribe to those events.

In this chapter, we will learn about the amazing features that CDI provides to your applications, including:

- Creating and using CDI beans
- Providing different implementations to your bean
- Understanding and using bean scopes
- Injecting beans in other components in different ways
- Understanding and using producers, interceptors, and events

What's new in CDI 2.0?

Before version 2.0, the CDI API was limited only to the scope of Java EE. Now and with CDI 2.0, the community did great in extending the scope of CDI into Java SE. Yes, like Spring and Google Guice, you can now use CDI in nearly any Java application.

If you are familiar enough with CDI, let's take a look at the new features that were added in CDI 2.0:

- CDI support in Java SE
- Ability to order events
- Asynchronous event
- Configurators for major SPI elements
- Possibility to configure or veto observer methods
- Add built-in annotation literals
- Make it possible to apply interceptors on producers
- Alignment on Java 8 features (streams, lambdas, repeating qualifiers)

 If you are not familiar with the CDI API, don't worry. Most of the terms mentioned in this section are going to be discussed throughout the rest of the chapter.

Creating your first CDI bean

A CDI bean is an application component that encapsulates some business logic. Beans can be used either by some Java code or by the unified EL (expression language used in JSP and JSF technologies). Beans' life cycles are managed by the container and can be injected into other beans. All you need to do to define a bean is to write a POJO and declare it to be a CDI bean. To declare that, there are two primary approaches:

- Using annotations
- Using the beans.xml file

Both ways should work; however, folks prefer using annotations over XML as it's handy and included in the actual coding context. So, why is XML just over there? Well, that's because annotations are relatively new in Java (released in Java 5). Until they were introduced, there was no other way in Java than XML to provide configuration information to your application server. And since then, it continued to be just another way, alongside the annotations approach.

Moreover, if both are used together, XML is going to override annotations. Some developers and application administrators tend to perform temporary changes or hot-fixes sometimes, by overriding some hard-coded programmatic configuration values, using external XML files. It worth mentioning that this approach is not a recommended way to actually deploy things into your production.

In all of the coming examples, we are going to use the annotations approach. However, in the *Using interceptors* section, a usage to the beans.xml file will be required and used in one example. Now, let's start our first example and define our first CDI bean:

First CDI bean

In this example, we are going to do two steps:

- Defining a CDI bean
- Injecting and using the CDI bean

Start the first step by creating a new Java class with the name `MyPojo`, and then write the following code:

```
@Dependent
public class MyPojo
    public String getMessage() {
        return "Hello from MyPojo !";
    }
}
```

In the previous code snippet, we have written our first CDI bean. As you likely noticed, the bean is nothing more than a plain old Java object, annotated with the `@Dependent` annotation. This annotation declares that our POJO is a CDI component, which is called the dependent scope. The dependent scope tells the CDI context that whenever we request an injection to this bean, a new instance will be created. The list of the other available scopes of CDI beans will be shown later, in the *Using scopes* section.

Now, let's move forward to the next step: injecting our baby CDI bean into another component. We are going to use a servlet as an example to this. Create a servlet named `ExampleServlet` and write the following code:

```
@WebServlet(urlPatterns = "/cdi-example-1")
public class ExampleServlet extends HttpServlet {

    @Inject
    private MyPojo myPojo;
    @Override
    protected void doGet(HttpServletRequest req, HttpServletResponse resp)
            throws ServletException, IOException {
        resp.getOutputStream().println(myPojo.getMessage());
    }

}
```

As you can see, we have used the `@Inject` annotation to obtain an instance to the `MyPojo` class. Now run the application, and visit the following URL: `http://localhost:8080/EnterpriseApplication1-war/cdi-example-1`.

You should see a page with the following text:

```
Hello from MyPojo !
```

Congratulations! You have just created and used your first CDI bean. Although the previous example looks trivial, and it seems we did nothing more than create a new instance of a class (could be much easier to use Java's new keyword, right?). However, by reading the following sections, you will encounter more CDI features that will attract you to the CDI API.

Providing alternative implementations to your bean

One of the greatest features of CDI is that you can provide two or more different implementations to the same bean. This is very useful if you wish to do one of the following:

- Handling client-specific business logic that is determined at runtime. For example, providing different payment mechanisms for a purchase transaction.
- Supporting different versions for different deployment scenarios. For example, providing an implementation that handles taxes in the USA, and another one for Europe.
- Easier management for test-driven development. For example, you can provide a primary implementation for production, and another mocked one for testing.

To do that, we should first rewrite our bean as an abstract element (abstract class or interface) and then we will be able to provide different implementations according to the basic OOP principles. Let's rewrite our bean to be an interface as follows:

```
public interface MyPojo {
    String getMessage();
}
```

Next, we will create an implementation class to our new interface:

```
@Dependent
public class MyPojoImp implements MyPojo{

    @Override
    public String getMessage() {
        return "Hello CDI 2.0 from MyPojoImp";
    }
}
```

Now, without any modifications to the servlet class, we can test re-run our example; it should give the following output:

```
Hello from MyPojoImp !
```

What happened at runtime? The container has received your request to inject a MyPojo instance; since the container has detected your annotation over an interface, not a class stuffed with an actual implementation, it has started looking for a concrete class that implements this interface. After that, the container has detected the MyPojoImp class that satisfies this criterion. Therefore, it has instantiated and injected it for you.

Now, let's go on with the critical part of the story, which is providing one more different implementations. For that, of course, we will need to create a new class that implements the MyPojo interface. Let's create a class called AnotherPojoImp as follows:

```
@Dependent
public class AnotherPojoImp implements MyPojo{

    @Override
    public String getMessage() {
        return "Hello CDI 2.0 from AnotherPojoImp";
    }
}
```

Seems simple, right? But if you checked our servlet code again, and if you were in the container shoes, how would you be able to determine which implementation should be injected at runtime? If you tried to run the previous example, you will end up with the following exception:

```
Ambiguous dependencies for type MyPojo with qualifiers @Default
```

We have an ambiguity here, and there should have some mean to specify which implementation version that should be used at runtime. In CDI, this is achieved by using qualifiers, which will be the topic of the next section.

Using qualifiers

A qualifier is a user-defined annotation that is used to tell the container which version of the bean implementation we wish to use at runtime. The idea of qualifiers is too simple; we define a qualifier, and then we annotate both the bean and injection point with this qualifier.

Let's define our first qualifier for the newly created bean implementation and create a new annotation with the following code:

```
@Qualifier
@Retention(RUNTIME)
@Target({TYPE, METHOD, FIELD, PARAMETER})
public @interface AnotherImp {

}
```

As you see, the qualifier is a custom-defined annotation, which itself is annotated with the `@Qualifier` annotation. `@Qualifier` tells the container that this annotation will act as a qualifier, while `@Retention(RUNTIME)` tells the JVM that this annotation should be available for reflection use at runtime, this way the container can check for this annotation at runtime. `@Target{TYPE, METHOD, FIELD, PARAMETER}` tells the compiler that this annotation can be used on types, methods, fields, and parameters. Anyway, the `@Qualifier` annotation is the key annotation here.

I have summarized the annotations that we have just mentioned in this table, to make it clearer:

Annotation	Description
@Qualifier	Tells CDI that this annotation is going to be used to distinguish between different implementations to the same interface.
@Retention(RUNTIME)	Tells JVM that this annotation is intended to be used in runtime. Required for qualifiers.
@Target({TYPE, METHOD, FIELD, PARAMETER})	Tells JVM that this annotation can be used on the mentioned syntax elements.

Now, let's go to the next step; we will add the `@AnotherImp` annotation to `AnotherPojoImp` as follows:

```
@Dependent
@AnotherImp
public class AnotherPojoImp implements MyPojo{

    @Override
    public String getMessage() {
        return "Hello from AnotherPojoImp";
    }
}
```

The annotation's role here is that it tells the container that this version of the class is called `AnotherImp`. Now we can reference this version by modifying the servlet as follows:

```
@WebServlet(urlPatterns = "/cdi-example")
public class ExampleServlet extends HttpServlet {

    @Inject @AnotherImp
    private MyPojo myPojo;
    ...
}
```

Run the example, and you should see the following:

Hello from AnotherPojoImp

But how can we reference the original implementation `MyPojoImp`? There are two options available to do that:

- Defining another qualifier for `MyPojoImp`, like the earlier example
- Using the default qualifier

The default qualifier, as the name suggests, is the default one for any CDI bean that has not been explicitly qualified. Although an explicit declaration for the default qualifier is considered redundant and useless, it's possible to explicitly declare your CDI bean as a default one by using the `@Default` annotation, as shown in the following revision to the `MyPojoImp` class:

```
@Default
@Dependent
public class MyPojoImp implements MyPojo{
    ...
}
```

Again, `@Default` is redundant, but you should consider its existence even if you have not explicitly declared it. Now, to reference the `MyPojoImp` from the servlet, we will rewrite it as follows:

```
@WebServlet(urlPatterns = "/cdi-example")
public class ExampleServlet extends HttpServlet {

    @Inject @Default
    private MyPojo myPojo;
    ...
}
```

This way, the original `MyPojoImp` implementation will be injected instead. And likewise, we can eliminate the `@Default` annotation, as the default implementation will be used by default!

Specifying a bean scope

CDI beans, according to the specification, are described to be *contextual*. By contextual it's meant that each CDI bean has a well-defined scope that it lives in. A scope describes the lifetime of the bean, that is, when the CDI bean shall be created and when it shall be destroyed. To make this more clear, consider the earlier examples where we have injected our beans into a servlet. The question is: will I obtain the same instance of the bean each time I run the example? Or will I obtain a new instance each time? Or one instance per user? Or what? The basic answer to all these questions, is specifying our bean scope.

One of the most popular examples of a bean scope that I'm pretty sure you have a prior knowledge of the singleton pattern. In this pattern, some class is supposed to have one, and only one, an instance of it in runtime. It should be created once, the first time it's required for usage, and destroyed whenever it's no longer useful or on the termination of our application. Such a pattern is one of our options when specifying the bean's scope property.

In the following list, we will list all available CDI scopes, alongside their annotation used, and the duration it lives in:

Scope	Annotation	Duration
Request	@RequestScoped	A user's interaction with a web application in a single HTTP request.
Session	@SessionScoped	A user's interaction with a web application across multiple HTTP requests.
Application	@ApplicationScoped	Shared state across all users' interactions with a web application (follows the singleton pattern).
Dependent	@Dependent	The default scope if none is specified; it means that an object exists to serve exactly one client (bean) and has the same life cycle as that client (bean).
Conversation	@ConversationScoped	A user's interaction with a servlet, including JavaServer Faces applications. The conversation scope exists within developer-controlled boundaries that extend it across multiple requests for long-running conversations. All long-running conversations are scoped to a particular HTTP servlet session and may not cross session boundaries.

- **Request Scope:** By using the request -scope, a new instance of the bean is created for each:

  - Request to the servlet, JSP, or JSF page
  - Call to remote EJB
  - Call to a web service

If multiple instances of the bean are injected by other beans, only one instance of the request-scoped bean is really created within the boundary of the user request in the cases we just listed and will be destroyed by the end of the user request. The following example shows how to make a CDI bean request-scoped:

```
@RequestScoped
public class MyPojo { ... }
```

- **Session scope:** By using the session-scope, a new instance of the bean is created for each user session. If multiple instances of the bean are injected by other beans, only one instance of the session-scoped bean is really created within the boundary of the user's HTTP session and will be destroyed by the expiration of the user's session. The following example shows how to make a CDI bean session-scoped:

```
@RequestScoped
public class MyPojo { ... }
```

- **Application scope:** By using the application-scope, only one instance of the bean is created for the entire application. If multiple instances of the bean are injected by other beans, only one instance of the application-scoped bean is really created globally within the entire application and will be destroyed when the application shuts down. The following example shows how to make a CDI bean application-scoped:

```
@RequestScoped
public class MyPojo {
```

- **Dependent scope:** By using the dependent-scope, a new instance of the bean is created for each injection point. If multiple instances of the bean are injected by other beans, a new instance of the dependent-scoped bean is really created within the boundary of the scope of the owner's bean, and will be destroyed with it. Instances will never be shared across different injection points. The following example shows how to make a CDI bean session-scoped:

```
@RequestScoped
public class MyPojo { ... }
```

- **Conversation scope:** By using the conversation-scope, a new instance of the bean is created for each maintained conversation. Conversations are introduced in JSF 2, and is out of the scope of this book.

Injecting beans

As you saw in previous examples, the @Inject annotation allows us to inject a bean as a field in another bean during its instantiation. However, the use of @Inject is not limited to fields only, as there are three valid mechanisms for injecting CDI beans:

- Direct field injection
- Bean constructor parameter injection
- Initializer method parameter injection

Direct field injection

Direct field injection is almost the easiest and most common mechanism for injecting CDI beans. By direct field injection, we mean that we define the injection point as an instance variable within another bean, then we use the @Inject annotation to request dependency injection. We have already used this mechanism in previous examples, so just to recall its code:

```
@Dependent
public class AnotherPojo {

    @Inject
    private MyPojo myPojo;

    . . .
}
```

Bean constructor parameter injection

Constructor injection is another mechanism for injecting CDI beans. By bean constructor parameter injection, we can use constructor parameters as injection points for our CDI beans. One major advantage of constructor injection is that it allows the bean to be immutable.

Look at the following `MyPojo` bean:

```
@Dependent
public class MyPojo {
    public String getMessage() {
        return "Hello from MyPojo!";
    }
}
```

We will get it injected using constructor parameters in `AnotherPojo`:

```
@Dependent
public class AnotherPojo {
    private MyPojo myPojo;
    @Inject
    public AnotherPojo(MyPojo myPojo) {
        this.myPojo = myPojo;
    }
    public String getMessage() {
        return myPojo.getMessage();
    }
}
```

As you can see, the `AnotherPojo`'s constructor is annotated with `@Inject`; this tells the container that this constructor holds parameters of injection points, which need to be satisfied during bean instantiation. Note that only one constructor can be used as an injection point in CDI beans.

Initializer method parameter injection

Initializer method parameter injection is a mechanism for injecting CDI beans, where a method is marked with `@Inject` to be called by the container in order to inject the required CDI bean. Here, we will show the previous example rewritten to use the initializer method parameter injection mechanism rather than the constructor parameter injection:

```
@Dependent
public class AnotherPojo {
    private MyPojo myPojo;
    @Inject
    public void setMyPojo(MyPojo myPojo) {
        this.myPojo = myPojo;
    }
    public String getMessage() {
```

```
        return myPojo.getMessage();
    }
}
```

Using producers

As shown earlier, a bean can have different alternatives, by introducing one interface and providing different implementations, each with a different qualifier. When injecting a reference to this interface in another bean, you can annotate your injection point with the qualifier for the implementation you desire. One interesting question is, can we specify which implementation to inject according to some runtime parameters, such as a user-specified choice?

For example, suppose a user is engaged in a payment workflow process. The first step is that the user will choose which payment method they prefer and where the next step they will actually perform the payment transaction. Suppose you have a PaymentStrategy interface with different bean implementations for a credit card, PayPal, and check payment strategies. Can we specify which bean implementation to reference according to the user choice? The answer is yes! This is called runtime polymorphism, and it can be achieved using producers.

A producer is a method that acts as a source of CDI beans. Consider the following example for a bean with different implementations:

```
public interface PaymentStrategy { ... }

public class CreditCardPaymentStrategy implements PaymentStrategy{ ...
}

public class CheckPaymentStrategy implements PaymentStrategy{ ... }

public class PayPalPaymentStrategy implements PaymentStrategy{ ... }
```

Let's define a Preferences bean. The preferences bean will act as a representation for the user-chosen preferences, and will include a producer method as follows:

```
@SessionScoped
public class Preferences implements Serializable {

    public static final int CREDIT_CARD = 0;
    public static final int CHECK = 1;
    public static final int PAYPAL = 2;
    private int paymentStrategy = ...;
```

```
@Produces
@Preferred
public PaymentStrategy getPaymentStrategy() {

    switch (paymentStrategy) {

        case CREDIT_CARD:
            return new CreditCardPaymentStrategy();

        case CHECK:
            return new CheckPaymentStrategy();

        case PAYPAL:
            return new PayPalPaymentStrategy();

        default:
            return null;

    }
  }
}
```

The `getPaymentStrategy` method is annotated with a `@Produces` annotation and this is called a `producer` method. It returns an instance for a `PaymentStrategy` implementation. The `@Preferred` annotation is a qualifier that will be used when injecting a reference to our bean, as follows:

```
@Qualifier
@Retention(RUNTIME)
@Target({TYPE, METHOD, FIELD, PARAMETER})
public @interface Preferred { }
```

Now, assume you have injected a reference to a `PaymentStrategy` as follows:

```
@Inject @Preferred PaymentStrategy paymentStrategy;
```

The method will run and detect which choice was made by the user for their preferred payment strategy, and, will return the appropriate implementation. The `producer` method technique is really useful when you need to choose one implementation in runtime according to a given parameter. However, there are other cases when using the producer method is useful, such as:

- You need to inject objects that are not real CDI beans
- You need to satisfy some initial values for your bean and/or performing some initial operations

Scope of producer methods

By default, producer methods run in the @Dependent scope; this means that each time an instance is requested to be injected within any context, a new instance of the bean will be created. However, you can customize this, by annotating your producer method with a scope annotation, as in the following example:

```
@SessionScoped
public class Preferences implements Serializable {
    ...
    @Produces
    @Preferred
    @RequestScoped
    public PaymentStrategy getPaymentStrategy() { ... }
}
```

In this example, only one instance of the PaymentStrategy bean will be instantiated per user request.

Injection into the producer methods

In the previous example, we have instantiated our bean inside the producer method using the Java new keyword. This is useful, as mentioned earlier when we need to use plain Java objects as CDI beans. However, if we want to make use of great CDI features, such as dependency injection and interceptors, we need to return a real CDI bean. To do this, we will rewrite our producer method as follows:

```
@SessionScoped
public class Preferences implements Serializable {
    ...
    @Produces
    @Preferred
    @RequestScoped
    public PaymentStrategy getPaymentStrategy(CreditCardPaymentStrategy ccps,
            CheckPaymentStrategy cps,
            PayPalPaymentStrategy ppps) {
        switch (paymentStrategy) {
        case CREDIT_CARD:
            return ccps;

        case CHECK:
            return cps;
```

```
        case PAYPAL:
            return ppps;

        default:
            return null;
        }
    }
}
```

In this example, we have provided the `producer` method with three parameters of the three possible implementations of the `PaymentStragey`. Yes, this is dependency injection! The container will inject three instances of the different available payment strategies, and then you will return one of the user choices. The difference here is that the returned bean will be created using the container, rather than Java's new keyword, and hence, it will utilize all the great services provided to CDI beans.

Using interceptors

Interceptors, as the name suggests, are methods that intercept other methods. With interceptors, you can write one method that will always run before one or other methods of your choice. Interceptors are useful when you are required to implement some cross-cutting concern, which should take kind of a global effect on some other scenarios. For example, suppose you want to log each method call in a payment processor bean, so you can later check what really happened during runtime in production. The direct mechanism to implement this is to write a logging function, then call it in each method in the payment processing bean. Although this seems simple, it's really redundant with the existence of interceptors. With interceptors, you can write your logging function once, and attach it with all other methods that you need to associate logging with. Interceptors also allow you to access the original method invocation context; this means that you can access parameters passed to the original method. Moreover, interceptors enable you to take control of the invocation itself, such as blocking the method invocation or even altering the return value.

Interceptors in CDI are a direct implementation to the aspect-oriented programming technique, you can also think of interceptors — recalling knowledge you may have with the servlets APIs, such as filters you map to servlets or JSPs. Filters intercept HTTP requests, and so do interceptors on CDI methods.

Common use cases of interceptors are:

- Logging
- Profiling
- Transaction management
- Authorization

Let's define our first CDI interceptor. Write a class called `MyInterceptor` with the following code:

```
public class MyInterceptor {

    @AroundInvoke
    public Object interceptMethod(InvocationContext ctx) throws
Exception {
        Object retValue = ctx.proceed();
        return "Intercepted! " + retValue;
    }
}
```

`interceptMethod()`, annotated with `@AroundInvoke`, is the method that is going to intercept some other methods. `@AroundInvoke` tells the container that this method is an intercepting one, which will always run each time before some other methods get executed upon a user call.

 We are going to define which other methods should be intercepted by this, in a later step.

In this intercepting method, you can do some pre and/or post operations, handle parameter's values, alter the return value, and even ban the original method call itself! The `InvocationContext` parameter is the object that you can use to retrieve the original method call information, and the most important part, proceeding with the original method call. The `proceed()` method in the `InvocationContext` object is used to

proceed the method call to the original one; note that if you did not call it, the intercepted method itself will not be called.

The next step is to associate this interceptor with some other methods. Recalling the `MyPojo` example, we will use the `@Interceptors` annotation to associate `MyInterceptor` with the `getMessage` method as follows:

```
@Dependent
public class MyPojo {

    @Interceptors(MyInterceptor.class)
    public String getMessage() {
        return "Hello from MyPojo!";
    }
```

By annotating the `getMessage()` method with the `@Interceptors` annotation, we tell the container that we wish to intercept the `getMessage()` method with the `MyInterceptor` interceptor. This means that whenever a call to `getMessage()` is performed, `interceptMethod` (annotated with `@AroundInvoke` in the `MyIntercrptor` class) will be called.

Now, if we injected the `MyPojo` bean in our example servlet, and tried to print the `getMessage()` return value, we would get the following output:

Intercepted! Hello from MyPojo!

As you see, `interceptMethod` has called the original method, read its return value, altered it, and then returned it to us, prefixed with the string `Intercepted!`.

You can also apply an interceptor to a complete class, by annotating the class itself with the `@Interceptors` annotation as follows:

```
@Dependent
@Interceptors(MyInterceptor.class)
public class MyPojo {

    public String getMessage1() {
        return "MyPojo first message!";
    }

    public String getMessage2() {
        return "MyPojo second message!";
    }
}
```

Now, all the methods in the `MyPojo` bean are intercepted using the `MyInterceptor` annotation. When trying to call any of them, the `interceptMethod` will intercept and produce the desired effect. Let's try to use `MyPojo` from our example servlet:

```java
@WebServlet(urlPatterns = "/cdi-example")
public class ExampleServlet extends HttpServlet {

    @Inject
    private MyPojo myPojo;
    @Override
    protected void doGet(HttpServletRequest req, HttpServletResponse resp)
            throws ServletException, IOException {
        resp.getOutputStream().println(myPojo.getMessage1());
        resp.getOutputStream().println(myPojo.getMessage2());
    }

}
```

This will be the output, as expected:

```
Intercepted! MyPojo first message!
Intercepted! MyPojo second message!
```

Interceptor types

One of the interesting features in CDI is that we can introduce interceptors using qualifiers. Let's define one interceptor called `LoggedInterceptor`, which is supposed to perform logging functionalities on a big set of CDI beans in some enterprise application:

```java
@Interceptor
@Logged
public class LoggedInterceptor {

    @AroundInvoke
    public Object interceptMethod(InvocationContext ctx) throws
Exception {
        Object retValue = ctx.proceed();
        return "intercepted " + retValue;
    }
}
```

Note that in this example, we have annotated the interceptor with the `@Logged` annotation. This is a qualifier annotation that we will define as shown earlier, in the *Using qualifiers* section, as follows:

```
@InterceptorBinding
@Target({TYPE, METHOD})
@Retention(RUNTIME)
public @interface Logged {
}
```

By annotating `LoggedInterceptor` with the qualifier `@Logged`, we can later annotate any CDI bean with the `@Logged` qualifier, to tell the container that we wish to use the `LoggedInterceptor` with that CDI bean, as follows:

```
@Dependent
@Logged
public class MyPojo { ... }
```

This is equivalent to the previous example, where we annotated `MyPojo` with the `@Interceptors` annotation. However, by using the qualifier rather than the interceptor class itself, we have abstracted `MyPojo` from the real interceptor implementation, and thus we can later alter this class type, or replace it among deployment modes (production or testing).

All CDI interceptors defined in this way are disabled by default. To make them enabled, you should define a `WEB-INF/beans.xml` file as the final step, with the following XML code:

```
<?xml version="1.0" encoding="UTF-8"?>
<beans xmlns="http://xmlns.jcp.org/xml/ns/javaee"
       xmlns:xsi="http://www.w3.org/2001/XMLSchema-instance"
       xsi:schemaLocation="http://xmlns.jcp.org/xml/ns/javaee
http://xmlns.jcp.org/xml/ns/javaee/beans_1_1.xsd"
       bean-discovery-mode="annotated">
    <interceptors>
        <class>com.example6.LoggedInterceptor</class>
    </interceptors>
</beans>
```

Note that without defining the interceptor in `beans.xml`, our example will not work as expected.

We can also apply qualified interceptors on singular methods as follows:

```
@Dependent
public class MyPojo {

    @Logged
    public String getMessage1() {
        return "MyPojo first message!";
    }
    ...
}
```

Using events

Events, as you may know, are runtime incidents that you do care about. CDI provides a loosely coupled model, following the observer design pattern, which allows you to fire an event from a CDI bean, and handling the event from one or more other CDI beans. The key advantages of the CDI events model are:

- Event producers and observers are decoupled from each other
- Observers can define selectors to limit the set of events they consume
- Observers are aware of database transactions and can consume events according to transaction states

In our booking application, we are going to use events in order to notify end users by email with either the success or failure of their booking operations, without tightly coupling the mailing code with the business logic of the booking itself.

Let's start by defining our booking database model; in the next chapter, this will be persisted in a relational database:

```
public class Booking {

    private long id;
    private long cinemaId;
    private long slotId;
    private long filmId;
    private List<Long> seatIds;
    private BigDecimal amountPaid;

    public Booking() {
    }

    public Booking(long id, long cinemaId, long slotId, long filmId,
```

```
      List<Long> seatIds, BigDecimal amountPaid) {
            this.id = id;
            this.cinemaId = cinemaId;
            this.slotId = slotId;
            this.filmId = filmId;
            this.seatIds = seatIds;
            this.amountPaid = amountPaid;
      }

      // getter and setter methods

}
```

Next, we will implement a booking notifier bean, which will represent the observer object for the booking event. The role of this object is to receive a signal when a booking operation has been made, then it prepares and sends an email to the end user confirming with them the booking details. The real code of sending email will be shown in Chapter 9, *Sending Mails with JavaMail 1.6*. For now, we will log a message to the application server console. Create a class with the name BookingNotifier and write the following code:

```
@Dependent
public class BookingNotifier {

    public void onBooking(@Observes Booking booking) {
        System.out.println("New Booking with id " + booking.getId());
        // a notification mail should be sent to the user
    }
}
```

As you have just noticed, the observer is no more than a normal CDI bean. What is special to events here is that we used the @Observers annotation on a parameter of a plain Java method; this tells the container that this method is interested in receiving the events regarding booking objects.

Now, when will this event be fired? Another CDI bean, whose role will be to actually perform the booking operation, will ask to notify all interested objects, as in the following code:

```
@Dependent
public class BookingHandler {

    private @Inject @Any Event<Booking> bookingEvent;

    public void book(Booking booking) {
        // do booking
```

```
        bookingEvent.fire(booking);
    }
}
```

As you see, when the booking operation is performed, it will notify our observer about the booking incident, where it will take the appropriate action.

 Note that we can define more observer objects, and all of them will be invoked upon firing this event, which is the role of the @Any annotation.

Now, let's complete our example by writing a servlet that simulates a user booking operation:

```java
@WebServlet(urlPatterns = "/cdi-example")
public class ExampleServlet extends HttpServlet {

    @Inject
    private BookingHandler bookingHandler;

    @Override
    protected void doGet(HttpServletRequest req, HttpServletResponse resp)
            throws ServletException, IOException {
        Booking booking = new Booking(1234, 1, 122, 241, (List<Long>)
Arrays.asList(1L, 2L, 3L), new BigDecimal("123"));
        bookingHandler.book(booking);
    }

}
```

By running the previous example, the output will be as follows:

```
New Booking with id 1234
Qualifying Events
```

Events can also be qualified, so we can propagate our event to a bean that is interested in a specific aspect of the event. Let's extend our example to design two types of events related to the booking operation, one for success, and the other for failure. There will be a bean that will react to the success event, where another one will react to the failure. We will define two qualifiers as follows:

```java
@Qualifier
@Retention(RUNTIME)
@Target({TYPE, METHOD, FIELD, PARAMETER})
public @interface Success {}
```

```
@Qualifier
@Retention(RUNTIME)
@Target({TYPE, METHOD, FIELD, PARAMETER})
public @interface Failure {

}
```

Then, we will replace @Any with the @Success annotation for the onBooking method, and write another one for @Failure as follows:

```
@Dependent
public class BookingNotifier {

    public void onBooking(@Observes @Success Booking booking) {
        System.out.println("New Booking with id " + booking.getId());
        // a notification mail should be sent to the user
    }

    public void onBookingFailed(@Observes @Failure Booking booking) {
        System.out.println("New Booking failed with id " +
booking.getId());
        // a notification mail should be sent to the user
    }
}
```

Now, we will inject two different event propagators in BookingHandler, one for the success, and the other for the failure, as follows:

```
@Dependent
public class BookingHandler {

    private @Inject @Success Event<Booking> bookingSuccessEvent;
    private @Inject @Failure Event<Booking> bookingFailedEvent;

    public void book(Booking booking) {
        try {
            // do booking
            bookingSuccessEvent.fire(booking);
        } catch (Exception e) {
            // booking failed
            bookingFailedEvent.fire(booking);
        }
    }
}
```

In the previous code, if the booking has been performed successfully, the success event will be fired, and the onBooking observer will be invoked. If some runtime errors occurred during the booking operation, the failure event will be fired, and the onBookingFailed observer will be invoked. This technique is very useful when we need to track different aspects of the same events in our enterprise application.

Summary

In this chapter, we have learned about dependency injection, which is one of the most important concepts in application development. We have explored the CDI 2.0 and the amazing features it provides and seen how to create and use CDI beans inside your application.

In the next chapter, we are going to make it much more interesting by learning database programming in JPA 2.1, where we will apply many topics that we have learned in this chapter, just over there. I hope you are ready!

3
Accessing the Database with JPA 2.1

The data access layer is the most fundamental part and the backbone of any enterprise application. The ultimate goal of any enterprise solution is to store and retrieve its data with respect to consistency, availability, and performance. A common problem arises when dealing with a relational database from an object-oriented system. All runtime data is represented as objects, where the real data is stored as rows in tables. When trying to save an object state into a row in a database table, or fetching some data from the database and wrapping the result back into an object again, a set of redundant programmatic statements should be written, which is very boring and actually old-school.

Object-to-relational mapping is a very common approach to overcoming this redundancy by providing a layer above the database access APIs, allowing developers to directly store and retrieve objects, and mapping their attributes directly to database tables and vice versa, providing a virtual object-oriented database interface for the actual relational data.

The Java Persistence API (JPA) does a great job at this by providing Java developers with all the required operations, mappings, and techniques for mapping objects into the relational database. In this chapter, we are going to learn how to use JPA for the following:

- Creating and using JPA entities
- Mapping entities to tables and columns
- Performing CRUD operations
- Mapping entity relationships
- Using the JPA query language and criteria APIs
- Mapping inheritance relationships

What's new in JPA 2.2?

For those who are familiar with JPA, let's first introduce the new features provided by JPA 2.2:

- Stream query results
- Repeatable annotations
- Java 8 date and time support
- CDI support in converters

Architecture

The Java persistence API is built around the following components:

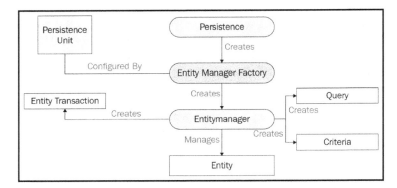

- **Persistence provider:** A persistence provider is a JPA implementation provided by a vendor. As with most Java APIs, JPA is a standard API, where a set of different actual implementations are available from different vendors. The persistence provider means the vendor of the actual implementation we are using.
- **Entities:** An entity is a class that represents a domain object in our enterprise application. From a JPA perspective, an entity is represented with a table in the database, and an instance of this entity represents a record in that table.

- **Entity managers:** An entity manager is an object that represents a connection to a database, and contains all methods for the different operations that can be performed with the database, such as inserting a new record, retrieving a single record, performing advanced queries, and so on.
- **Entity transaction:** An entity transaction represents a database transaction that can be either committed or rolled back according to the application state. Any update operations (insert, update, delete) should be performed within the boundaries of an entity transaction.
- **Query:** As the name suggests, a query is an object that is used to perform a database query! In addition to the regular SQL, JPA provides a custom query language (called JPQL) that can be used to perform queries exactly like SQL, but with object-oriented concepts.
- **Persistence unit:** A persistence unit is a group of entities involved in a persistence context. A persistence unit is specified using a configuration file (`persistence.xml`), describing connection information, entities involved, and other useful configurations.

Writing your first JPA application

Let's start learning JPA by writing a simple application that receives some movie data from the user through a web page interface, then saves the user input into a database table.

Step 1: Creating a data source

The first step is to define a data source inside the enterprise application. A data source represents a pool of JDBC connections to a specific database that will be used later by the persistence APIs. A data source is identified by a JNDI name, and includes JDBC connection information. To declare your data source in GlassFish, you should create a `glassfish-resources.xml` file in the `WEB-INF` folder for your project, as shown in the following file:

```
/WEB-INF/glassfish-resources.xml
<?xml version="1.0" encoding="UTF-8"?>
<!DOCTYPE resources PUBLIC "-//GlassFish.org//DTD GlassFish Application
Server 3.1 Resource Definitions//EN"
"http://glassfish.org/dtds/glassfish-resources_1_5.dtd">
<resources>
    <jdbc-connection-pool allow-non-component-callers="false"
associate-with-thread="false" connection-creation-retry-attempts="0"
connection-creation-retry-interval-in-seconds="10" connection-leak-
reclaim="false" connection-leak-timeout-in-seconds="0" connection-
```

```
validation-method="auto-commit" datasource-
classname="com.mysql.jdbc.jdbc2.optional.MysqlDataSource" fail-all-
connections="false" idle-timeout-in-seconds="300" is-connection-
validation-required="false" is-isolation-level-guaranteed="true" lazy-
connection-association="false" lazy-connection-enlistment="false"
match-connections="false" max-connection-usage-count="0" max-pool-
size="32" max-wait-time-in-millis="60000"
name="mysql_cinemasapp_rootPool" non-transactional-connections="false"
pool-resize-quantity="2" res-type="javax.sql.DataSource" statement-
timeout-in-seconds="-1" steady-pool-size="8" validate-atmost-once-
period-in-seconds="0" wrap-jdbc-objects="false">
        <property name="serverName" value="localhost"/>
        <property name="portNumber" value="3306"/>
        <property name="databaseName" value="cinemasapp"/>
        <property name="User" value="root"/>
        <property name="Password" value="root"/>
        <property name="URL"
value="jdbc:mysql://localhost:3306/cinemasapp?zeroDateTimeBehavior=conv
ertToNull"/>
        <property name="driverClass" value="com.mysql.jdbc.Driver"/>
    </jdbc-connection-pool>
    <jdbc-resource enabled="true" jndi-name="java:app/cinemasapp-ds"
object-type="user" pool-name="mysql_cinemasapp_rootPool"/>
</resources>
```

Step 2: Creating a persistence unit

A persistence unit in is named scope where we define persistence contextual details such as data source information, a list of entities to include (or exclude), and any other information that may be useful for the persistence provider to work. A persistence unit is identified by a unit name, and is created by defining the following file:

```
/META-INF/persistence.xml
<?xml version="1.0" encoding="UTF-8"?>
<persistence version="2.1"
xmlns="http://xmlns.jcp.org/xml/ns/persistence"
xmlns:xsi="http://www.w3.org/2001/XMLSchema-instance"
xsi:schemaLocation="http://xmlns.jcp.org/xml/ns/persistence
http://xmlns.jcp.org/xml/ns/persistence/persistence_2_1.xsd">
  <persistence-unit name="jpa-examplesPU" transaction-type="JTA">
    <jta-data-source>java:app/cinemasapp-ds</jta-data-source>
    <exclude-unlisted-classes>false</exclude-unlisted-classes>
    <properties>
      <property name="javax.persistence.schema-
generation.database.action" value="create"/>
    </properties>
```

```
        </persistence-unit>
    </persistence>
```

 Note that by setting the `exclude-unlisted-classes` property to false, all entity classes found by the persistence provider inside the WAR deployment file will be included in the context of the persistence unit.

Step 3: Creating an entity class

An entity class is the main player in a JPA application. It's a class that represents a table in the database, whose instances, in turn, represent rows inside this table. An entity class is no more than a POJO, annotated with `@Entity`, with a field elected as a primary key and annotated with `@Id`, as in the following example:

```java
Movie.java
@Entity
public class Movie {

    @Id
    @GeneratedValue
    private long id;
    private String title;

    public Movie() {
    }

    public long getId() {
        return id;
    }

    public void setId(long id) {
        this.id = id;
    }

    public String getTitle() {
        return title;
    }

    public void setTitle(String title) {
        this.title = title;
    }

}
```

Note that you do not have to create a corresponding table in the database yourself, as the persistence unit is declared with the `javax.persistence.schema-generation.database.action` property set to `create`, which means that the persistence provider is responsible for creating the table in the database, if it does not exist.

Step 4: Creating a data access object

Now to the key part, where we will mix the knowledge we learned in `Chapter 2`, *Dependency Injection Using CDI 2.0*, to use persistence APIs. As you may know, any data access layer includes what's called data access objects; those objects are responsible for performing basic data housekeeping operations such as inserting, retrieving, modifying, and deleting rows from the database.

To do this in JPA, we have to first obtain an instance of the persistence provider object that implements the fundamental JPA `EntityManager` interface. To obtain such an object, the following code is used:

```
EntityManagerFactory emf = Persistence.createEntityManagerFactory("jpa-examplesPU");
EntityManager em = emf.createEntityManager();
```

Using CDI, we can just inject an instance of the entity manager without all the hassle of manually obtaining that instance shown in the previous code excerpt; this is achieved using the `@PersistenceContext` annotation, which is equivalent to the `@Inject` annotation discussed in the previous chapter, but is different in that it's used specifically for entity managers and is passed the persistence unit name as shown in the following code:

```
@RequestScoped
public class MovieBean {

    @PersistenceContext(name = "jpa-examplesPU")
    private EntityManager entityManager;

}
```

Now, let's define an `insert` method that is used to insert a movie entity into the database:

```
@RequestScoped
@Transactional
public class MovieBean {

    @PersistenceContext(name = "jpa-examplesPU")
    private EntityManager entityManager;

    public void insert(Movie movie) {
```

```
            entityManager.persist(movie);
        }

    }
```

As you see, we have called the `persist` method, passing a movie instance, which will be inserted as a row in the database. Other entity managers methods and features will be discussed in future sections in greater detail.

But, what's the role of the `@Transactional` attribute? The `@Transactional` attribute defines an interceptor (remember this concept from the previous chapter?) which automates entity transactions on all the methods in the annotated bean. As mentioned earlier in the architecture section, all database transactions should be performed within the boundaries of an entity transaction. To do this programmatically, the following code should be written:

```
            entityManager.getTransaction().begin();
            entityManager.persist(movie);
            entityManager.getTransaction().commit();
```

If you are familiar with database transactions, there should be no problem with the previous code. We should start an active transaction before performing any database update operations, and at the end, we should commit out transaction. This is a very important concept in relational databases in order to keep the integrity of your data when performing a multi-step database operation, so that either all operations complete successfully upon reaching the commit statement, or nothing is applied at all if it failed to reach the commit statement as an exception occurred.

The transactional attribute on your CDI bean automates the previous code excerpt. You will never need to begin or commit your transactions, as all methods in a `@Transactional` bean will run within the boundary of an entity transaction. Moreover, if a `@Transactional` bean method calls `other` methods with nested database operations, all the database operations of the original or submethods will execute within the boundary of the same transaction. Transaction propagation is one of the most important features required in any enterprise application, and is achieved using the `@Transactional` attribute with zero code.

Now, let's write a servlet and a JSP to test our code:

```
            @WebServlet(urlPatterns = "/add-movie")
            public class AddMovieServlet extends HttpServlet{

                @Inject
                private MovieBean movieBean;
```

```java
@Override
protected void doPost(HttpServletRequest request,
HttpServletResponse response) throws ServletException, IOException {
        String movieTitle = request.getParameter("movie_title");
        Movie movie = new Movie();
        movie.setTitle(movieTitle);
        movieBean.insert(movie);
    }
}
```

Here is the JSP to test the code:

```html
<html>
    <head>
        <title>Add a New Movie</title>
        <meta charset="UTF-8">
    </head>
    <body>
        <h1>Add a New Movie</h1>
        <form action="./add-movie" method="POST">
            Title: <input name="movie_title" type="text"/><br/>
            <input type="submit" value="Add"/>
        </form>
    </body>
</html>
```

Run the JSP; the following page should be displayed:

Now, write a title, click **Add**, and then refer to the database. Your new entity should have been added successfully.

Congratulations! You have just written your first JPA application. In the following sections, we are going to study JPA in great detail.

Entities

An entity is a domain object that represents a business entity, and correspondingly, a record in a database table. An entity class should satisfy the following requirements:

- The class must be annotated with the `javax.persistence.Entity` annotation.
- The class must have a public or protected no-argument constructor. The class may have other constructors.
- The class must not be declared final. No methods or persistent instance variables may be declared final.
- If an entity instance is passed by value as a detached object, such as through a session bean's remote business interface, the class must implement the `Serializable` interface.
- Entities may extend both entity and non-entity classes, and non-entity classes may extend entity classes.
- Persistent instance variables must be declared private, protected, or package-private and can be accessed directly only by the entity class's methods. Clients must access the entity's state through accessor or business methods.

Entity mapping

One of the fundamental tasks in JPA development is to map your domain model entity classes to your database tables and columns. There are two approaches when you are going to design your entities and database in general:

- Designing entity classes and generating a database schema from them
- Designing database tables then implementing entity classes around them

The first approach is only valid and useful when you are starting your application from scratch. Beginning the design with entity classes makes it easier for you, as an application developer, to analyze and design your solution with object-oriented techniques. Note that this may be suitable only for small to medium-scale applications. In large-scale applications, there may be a big database design and implementation team who will take on the database responsibility. In such a case, you have to follow the second approach. Another common case is that the database may exist, as you are going to develop a new vertical application above an existing application, or you are revamping or migrating an existing system to newer technologies.

Anyways, by learning the basic mappings of JPA, you will be able to follow either of these approaches.

Primary keys

A primary key field is mapped by using the @Id annotation as in the following example:

```
@Entity
public class Movie {
    @Id
    private long id;
}
```

 Note that the primary key field itself should not be named Id; this is just a very common situation where we use a field with the name id as the primary key of our table. However, the primary key field can be named anything.

You can also use the primary key field on a getter method in the following example:

```
@Entity
public class Movie {
private long id;

    @Id
public long getId() {
        return id;
    }

}
```

The difference between the two approaches is that if you used the @Id annotation on a class field directly, the persistence provider will read all other mapping annotations from class fields. Otherwise, it will read all other mappings from the getter methods. You cannot mix annotations on both fields and getters, and the @Id annotation is a discriminator here. The choice between either approaches is the developer's preference. I personally prefer using field mapping in order to make all mapping information available at the beginning of the class.

Table mapping

By default, an entity class is mapped to a table with the same name as the class. However, there are cases when you need to modify this default name for one of the following reasons:

- You need to use a custom name for a neater database design.
- You have to map it to an existing table in a legacy database.
- Your entity name is a SQL reserved keyword, for example, User. You are forced to modify the table name, otherwise you will end up with a runtime error.

The @Table annotation is used to customize the table name as in the following example:

```
@Entity
@Table(name = "movies")
public class Movie {
    ...
}
```

Column mapping

By default, all fields (or getter methods, according to @Id place) are mapped as columns in the containing table, with a default name matching the field (or getter) name, and a default type matching its Java type, if you need to customize how a column is mapped in the database, as in the following code snippet:

```
@Entity
public class Movie {
    @Column(name = "movie_title")
    private String title;
    ....
}
```

In the previous example, we have customized the name of the title field to movie_title. Moreover, the previous example maps by default to the database type VARCHAR. As you know, VARCHAR types have a length. The default length of a VARCHAR field in JPA is 255, but you can customize this value by using the length attribute:

```
@Entity
public class Movie {
    @Column(name = "movie_title", length=100)
    private String title;
    ....
}
```

If you have a text type available in your database, you can also modify the default type by using the `columnDefinition` attribute:

```
@Entity
public class Movie {
    @Column(name = "movie_title", columnDefinition = "text")
    private String title;
    ....
}
```

Other attributes are available for the customization of table columns, as shown in the following table:

Name	Type	Description	Default
nullable	Boolean	Whether the database column is nullable.	FALSE
unique	Boolean	Whether the column is a unique key. This is a shortcut for the `UniqueConstraint` annotation at the table level and is useful for when the unique key constraint corresponds to only a single column. This constraint applies in addition to any constraint entailed by primary key mapping and to constraints specified at the table level.	FALSE
precision	int	The precision for a decimal (exact numeric) column applies only if a decimal column is used. Values must be set by developer if used when generating the DDL for the column.	0
scale	int	The scale for a decimal (exact numeric) column. Applies only if a decimal column is used.	0
insertable	Boolean	Whether the column is included in SQL `INSERT` statements generated by the persistence provider.	TRUE
updatable	Boolean	Whether the column is included in SQL `UPDATE` statements generated by the persistence provider.	TRUE

Date and time mapping

In a typical relational database, there are three basic data types for columns:

- Date
- Time
- Timestamp

All of these three data types are represented in Java as an instance of the `java.util.Date` class. To make this clear for mapping by the persistence provider, the `@Termporal` annotation should be used to identify which one of the three database types should be selected. The following example shows how the `@Temportal` annotation is used:

```
@Entity
public class Movie {
    @Temporal(TemporalType.DATE)
    private Date releaseDate;
}
```

The following values are available for the `@Termporal` annotation:

- `TemporalType.DATE`: Date-only values
- `TemporalType.TIME`: Time-only values
- `TemporalType.TIMESTAMP`: Date with time values

Ignoring properties

By default, all fields (or `getter` methods) are mapped to a table column. However, there are cases when you want to exclude some fields or `getter` methods in entity classes from being mapped to the database table. For example, you may include a variable that is calculated on the fly, such as the number of years elapsed since the production of the movie, which will be calculated at runtime, and makes no sense if included in the database itself. In such cases, the `@Transient` annotation is used to tell the persistence provider to prevent some fields or `getter` methods from being mapped to the database table, as in the following example:

```
@Entity
public class Movie {
    ....
    @Transient
    private Integer yearsOld;

    public int getYearsOld() {
        if (yearsOld == null) {
            yearsOld = (int) ((System.currentTimeMillis() -
            releaseDate.getTime())
/ 1000 / 60 / 60 / 24 / 365);
        }
        return yearsOld;
    }
}
```

In the previous example, the `yearsOld` field will not be mapped to the database, and its use in our application will be limited to a state variable supporting the lazy loading technique we have applied to the `getYearsOld` method.

Composite primary keys

As a primary key of a relational database table can be composite, you can also declare your entity's primary key as composite. To do this, you can simply annotate more than one field with the `@Id` annotation.

However, in order to retrieve an entity using its primary key with the entity manager's `find` method, you have to define what's called an `id` class and associate it with your entity. An instance of this `id` class will be used to look up single entities by their primary keys and retrieve them later. Let's go through the following example:

```
@Entity
@IdClass(MovieId.class)
public class Movie {

    @Id
    private String title;
    @Id
    private int productionYear;

    public Movie() {
    }

    // getters and setters here
}
```

As you can see, we have annotated two fields with the `@Id` annotation. Now, we have a composite primary key, consisting of the title and `productionYear` fields. Moreover, we have used the `@Id` class annotation in order to define an associated primary key class. The `id` class is a POJO that includes the fields of the composite primary key, as follows:

```
public class MovieId {

    private String title;
    private int productionYear;

    public MovieId() {
    }

    public MovieId(String title, int productionYear) {
```

```
        this.title = title;
        this.productionYear = productionYear;
    }
    // getters and setters here
}
```

Now, to be able to retrieve a movie entity using its primary key, we will be using an instance of this id class in order to define the primary key for the entity manager's find method. Note that we have included a constructor to initialize the composite fields for easier use:

```
following Movie m = entityManager.find(Movie.class, new MovieId("Beauty
and the Beans", 2017));
```

The id class in the previous example seems redundant, because we have defined the composite primary key fields twice, once in the entity class itself, and again in the id class. However, if you had not included an id class, you would have found something missing when using the entity manager's find method. That's because you need to specify the values of two fields, and there will be no Java way available rather than the id class!

However, if you are still feeling redundant, JPA uses the embedded id feature, which allows you to reuse the id class in defining the composite primary key fields for the entity itself. Let's try this in the following example:

```
@Entity
public class Movie {

    @EmbeddedId
    private MovieId movieId;

    public Movie() {
    }

    // getters and setters here

}
```

As you see, we have not included the title and productionYear fields themselves. Instead, we have included a field of type MovieId with those fields, which we have reused from the previous example. The @EmbeddedId annotation tells the JPA provider that we need to embed the contents of the MovieId class in the Movie entity class itself, imaging this as you have copied/pasted the contents from the MovieId class into the Movie class. Those fields will be merged as columns in the same Movie's table.

One more annotation will require to be added to the `MovieId` class, the `@Embeddable` annotation, as follows:

```
@Embeddable
public class MovieId {
    ....
}
```

Now we have achieved exactly the same results as in the previous example. We can still retrieve movies using the same line of code:

```
Movie m = entityManager.find(Movie.class, new MovieId("Beauty and the
Beans", 2017));
```

But using embedded ids, we have reused our `id` class, and included a single maintenance point in the composite `id`. In other words, to modify the set of fields composing the composite id, we will edit only the embedded `id` class, and no changes will be applied to the `movie` class in this case.

Embedded objects

There are cases when you need to separate some related entity fields in separate objects for the sake of a design decision. For example, for each movie there is a big set of attributes describing the movie entity. We may decide to separate them in a separate object, called `MovieInfo`. However, we do not want to separate them in a different table (as will be shown later in the relationships section). In this case, we need to only **embed** a set of fields in a different object to the entity itself, and include them as columns in the owner entity's table. This is called **embedding** objects in JPA. You will find the idea of embedded objects very similar to the embedded IDs shown earlier. Let's see an example of this:

```
@Entity
public class Movie {

    @Id
    @GeneratedValue
    private long id;
    private String title;
    @Embedded
    private MovieInfo movieInfo;

    public Movie() {
    }
```

```
        // getters and setters here
    }
```

In the previous code snippet, we used the @Embedded annotation to tell the JPA provider that the MovieInfo field should be embedded in the Movie entity. Now, let's see what the MovieInfo class looks like:

```
@Embeddable
public class MovieInfo {

    private long runtime;
    private String storyLine;
    private String country;
    private String language;

    public MovieInfo() {
    }


    // getters and setters here
}
```

In the previous code snippet, we annotated the MovieInfo class with the @Embeddable annotation, which tells the JPA provider that the MovieInfo class is embeddable within the context of our JPA application.

Now, let's see an example of how to persist an instance of the Movie class:

```
Movie movie = new Movie();
movie.setTitle("Beauty and the Beast");

MovieInfo movieInfo = new MovieInfo();
movieInfo.setStoryLine("A young prince, imprisoned in the form of a
beast, can be freed only by true love.");
movieInfo.setRuntime(129);
movieInfo.setLanguage("English");
movieInfo.setCountry("USA");

movie.setMovieInfo(movieInfo);
```

In the previous code snippet, we instantiated a separate MovieInfo object, setting its attributes with the desired values, then we associated it with an instance of the Movie class. After that, we can persist the Movie instance, where the MovieInfo attributes will be embedded within the Movie table.

Performing CRUD operations

In the following sections, we are going to learn how to use JPA for performing the four basic data access operations: creating, retrieving, updating, and deleting entities.

Managed versus detached entities

One of the most important concepts to understand about the JPA framework is that every entity has a state at each point during runtime. An entity can be in one of two states:

- **Managed:** A managed entity is one that is synchronized with the database; any changes in the entity state will be reflected in the database. In other words, the persistence provider is tracking a managed entity state, and keeps updating the database with any changes that occur to its state.
- **Detached:** A detached entity is one that is not synchronized with the database; any changes in the entity state will not be reflected to the database. The persistence provider does not track any changes that occur to the entity.

As you will see later, by performing the different CRUD operations supported by the entity manager, such as the persist operation mentioned in the earlier example, the entity state will change from one to the other. Take note of this concept, as this will totally affect your database operations.

Inserting a new record

The `persist` method is used to insert a new record in the database, as in the following example:

```
Movie m = new Movie(); // detached
// initialize the entity state
entityManager.persist(movie); // managed

m.setTitle("New Title");
```

When creating a new instance of the `Movie` class, the object is said to be in the detached mode, according to the JPA terminology. Detached mode describes that this entity is not connected with a database row yet.

When persisting the movie entity, a row will be inserted into the `Movie` table, with all the values we have initialized in the movie instance. After that, the movie entity will go to the managed mode. With the managed mode, the JPA tracks state changes for the movie instance when performing a database commit. In other words, modifying the entity attributes after that will take effect in the database within the bounds of a database transaction.

Retrieving an existing record

The `find` method is used to retrieve an entity from the database:

```
Movie m = entityManager.find(Movie.class, 1); // managed
```

The returned instance in this case is a managed instance. If you have made some changes, it will take effect in the database within the bounds of a database transactions, as discussed in the previous section. See the following example:

```
Movie m = entityManager.find(Movie.class, 1);
m.setTitle("New Title");
```

The new title will be applied to the entity's row in the database.

Updating an existing record

The `merge` method is used to update an entity in the database, using an unmanaged instance. See the following example:

```
Movie movie = entityManager.find(Movie.class, 1);
movie.setTitle("Modified title");
```

We have retrieved the movie, then made a change to its title, which will be applied as discussed earlier. Note that the `find` method returns null if no row really exists with the specified primary key.

However, there are cases when you need to update all the values for a row using an detached one. For example, after displaying the values for an existing movie in an edit page in the administration area, you will perform an update operation to all values when the user saves. The edit form will submit new values where you instantiate a detached entity, wraps the user's new values, then wants to perform an update operation.

In this case, the merge operation will do this for you. It takes an unmanaged entity, finds the matching one in the database using its primary key, then updates the values in the database using the given one. Let's see an example of this:

```
Movie movie = new Movie();
movie.setId(1);
movie.setTitle("Modified title");
entityManager.merge(movie);
```

As you see, we have created a new instance of `movie`, set its primary key to an existing one, set a new title for it, then passed it to the merge operation. The movie with `id` 1 in the database will be updated with the modified title. Note that the `merge` operation keeps the passed instance detached, so any further modification to this instance value after the merge operation will not be applied to the database in the boundaries of a database transaction. However, the `merge` method returns a managed instance, which you can use for this purpose, as in the following example:

```
    . . . .
Movie managed = entityManager.merge(movie);
        managed.setTitle("Even more modification");
```

The instance returned by the `merge` operation, which is a different one from the one we passed, will be managed, and your changes to it will apply within the boundaries of a database transaction.

However, there are cases where you want to modify only a single value of the database entity. In this case, the two approaches mentioned earlier will not be the best. For the find approach, you will have to perform a retrieval operation first before you modify, which means one extra hit to the database (in case the entity was not loaded already in the entity manager's context). And the merge approach will be not valid, as you still satisfy all the passed entity's attributes with the desired values, which is suitable only in cases where you need to modify all values at once, not a single one.

To do this, you can use the entity manager's `getReference` method. The `getReference` method seems like find at first sight, but it differs from find in that it returns a `proxy` object with no real data, rather than a real entity with all the real data. Examine the following example:

```
Movie movie = entityManager.getReference(Movie.class, 1);
```

The returned `movie` object is a proxy object, not the real one. The JPA provider will not look for the values in the database. In other words, no database hit will be performed in this step.

 Note that this `proxy` object is considered an entity in the managed state.

Now, let's extend our example to modify a single attribute:

```
Movie movie = entityManager.getReference(Movie.class, 1);
movie.setTitle("Modified Title");
```

Now, and within the boundaries of a database transaction, the new value will be applied to the database. The difference between this approach and the find approach is that in this approach we have hit the database only once, not twice.

Note that the `proxy` object can still be used to fetch data. If you try to print the title of this movie, it will be printed without a problem, and this is achieved by lazy loading. In other words, upon your request to get the title of the returned movie, an actual database hit will be performed to load this value, as in the following example:

```
Movie movie = entityManager.getReference(Movie.class, 1);
System.out.println(movie.getTitle());
```

Deleting a record

The `remove` method is used to delete an entity from the database, where a managed entity should be passed to the `remove` method. For example, to remove the movie with `id` 1, the following code could be used:

```
Movie movie = entityManager.find(Movie.class, 1);
entityManager.remove(this);
```

But in this case, we have hit the database twice, as shown in the previous section. Therefore, if we want to delete an entity without checking its values, we can use `getReference` instead to obtain the instance we wish to remove:

```
Movie movie = entityManager.getReference(Movie.class, 1);
entityManager.remove(this);
```

Detaching an entity

In some cases, you may have a managed instance that you need to stop synchronizing with the database. In JPA terminology, you need to detach this entity from the context of the entity manager. In this case, you can use the `detach` method, as shown in the following example:

```
Movie movie = entityManager.find(Movie.class, 1);
entityManager.detach(movie);
movie.setTitle("Not mofiied title!");
```

If you need to detach all loaded entities within the context of the entity manager, you can simply use the `clear` method:

```
entityManager.clear();
```

Mapping entity relationships

Database relationships are one of the most important concepts in relational databases. From an object-oriented programming perspective, database relationships are seen as an association relationship. An object may reference an instance of another class, or a list of instances of this class, and this is called association, or the has-a relationship in OOP, which maps directly to the concept of relational databases.

JPA provides a complete framework for mapping and using database relationships using object-oriented approaches. The rule of thumb is very easy: when an entity class references an instance (or a list of instances) of another entity class, this should be mapped to a database relationship. Four types of relationship exist in JPA:

- One-to-one
- One-to-many
- Many-to-many
- Many-to-one

Before moving on, let's refresh our concepts about these relationships. From an object-oriented perspective, when an entity references another singular entity, this is a to-one relationship, which could be either one-to-one or many-to-one. If an entity references a list (or set) of another entities, this is a to-many relationship, which could be either many-to-many or one-to-many. It's sometimes tricky to pick the right relationship; when it's a singular relationship, when to choose one-to-one, and when to choose many-to-one ? And the same for plural relationships; is it one-to-many, or many-to-many ?

To pick the right one, you should always examine the reverse part of the relationship. For example, for each movie, there is a producer, therefore the relationship can be either one-to-one or many-to-one. To pick one of the two, you should ask the following question: for each producer, how many movies may he produce ? The answer is, for sure, many ! So, this relationship is many-to-one, not one-to-one. Another example: for each movie, there is a set of contributing actors. So, for each actor, how many movies can he/she contribute to? The answer is many ! So, this relationship is many-to-many. But, recalling the movie info example from the embedded entities section, if for each movie, there is movie info (let's use relationships rather than embedded objects), can the same movie info describe another movie ? The answer is no! So, this is a one-to-one relationship, as the other party is exclusively related to the owner.

Moreover, from an object-oriented perspective, an association relationship can either be unidirectional or bidirectional. A unidirectional relationship applies, for example, when a movie references a producer, where the producer does not reference his/her movies. A bidirectional relationship, on the other hand, applies when a producer also references his/her movies. Although the bidirectional relationships concept does not exist in relational databases, it exists in object-oriented programming and the JPA framework.

Now, let's study JPA relationships in detail in the following sections.

Many-to-one relationships

Suppose we have the following `Producer` entity:

```
@Entity
public class Producer {
    @Id
    @GeneratedValue
    private long id;
    private String name;

    public Producer() {
    }

    // getters and setters here
}
```

And we have a movie entity that references an instance of the producer entity. A many-to-many relationship exists, and should be mapped using the `@ManytoOne` annotation as follows:

```
@Entity
public class Movie {

    ...
    @ManyToOne
    private  Producer producer;
    ...
}
```

To use this relationship with an existing producer, we should first fetch the producer from the database, assign it to our movie, then persist the new movie in the database, as shown in the following code snippet:

```
Query query = entityManager.createQuery
                ("SELECT p FROM Producer p WHERE p.name=:name");
query.setParameter("name", "Walt Disney");
Producer producer = (Producer) query.getSingleResult();

Movie movie = new Movie();
movie.setTitle("Beauty and the Beast");
movie.setProducer(producer);

entityManager.persist(movie);
```

Many-to-many relationships

Suppose we have the following `Actor` entity:

```
@Entity
public class Actor {
    @Id
    @GeneratedValue
    private long id;
    private String name;
    private boolean gender;

    public Actor() {
    }

    // getters and setters here
}
```

And we have a movie entity that references a list of those actors. Therefore, a many-to-many relationship exists, and should be mapped using the `@ManyToMany` annotation as follows:

```
@Entity
public class Movie {

    ...
    @ManyToMany
    private List<Actor> actors = new ArrayList<>();
    ...
}
```

To use this relationship with a list of existing actors, we should first fetch the actors from the database, assign them to our movie, then persist the new movie in the database, as shown in the following code snippet:

```
List<Actor> someActors = ....; // fetch them from the database

Movie movie = new Movie();
movie.setTitle("Beauty and the Beast");
movie.getAcotrs().addAll(someActors);
entityManager.persist(movie);
```

Bidirectional relationships

As mentioned earlier, a bidirectional relationship exists when both parties reference each other in any type of relationship. Sometimes, it's useful to implement a bidirectional relationship to make it easier when fetching some information related to the entity. For example, in a movie page, we for sure will need to show the name of its producer, which is already contained in the `movie` object as the owner of the relationship. However, when a user clicks the producer page, we may also want to list all the movies produced by this producer alongside other information related to this producer. Instead of querying them in another statement, we can apply the bidirectional relationship so we always have the movie information related to each `producer` object when fetching it from the database.

Recalling the movie-producer relationship, let's apply the reverse relationship as follows:

```
@Entity
public class Producer {
    ....
    @OneToMany
    private List<Movie> movies = new ArrayList<>();
```

```
        public Producer() {
        }

        // getters and setters here
    }

@Entity
public class Movie {

        . . .
        @ManyToOne(mappedBy="movies")
        private  Producer producer;
        . . .
    }
```

As you see, we declared a list of movies in the `producer` entity; this is the OOP reverse association relationship. This is directly a one-to-many relationship in JPA, and therefore we have used the `@OneToMany` annotation. To tell the JPA provider that this is a reverse relationship with the movie's one, and not a new database relationship, we have used the `mappedBy` attribute in the `@ManyToOne` annotation in the `Movie` entity. The value of the `mappedBy` attribute is the name of the attribute on the reverse side, which represents the reverse relationship, in this case, movies. Note that the `mappedBy` attribute is not available in the `@OneToMany` annotation.

Cascading

Suppose you have a relationship between two entities, a `Movie` and a `Producer`, with a many-to-one relationship between them as follows:

```
@Entity
public class Producer {
private List<Movie> movies = new ArrayList<>();

    . . .
}

@Entity
public class Movie {

    . . .
    @ManyToOne
    private  Producer producer;
    . . .
}
```

Now, if we have created an instance of movie, then an instance of producer, then passed the producer to the movie reference and tried to persist the `movie`, will the operation completes successfully ?

Look at the following code:

```
Movie movie = new Movie();
Producer producer = new Producer();
// filling stating variables
movie.setProducer(producer);
entityManager.persist(movie);
```

Does persisting the movie persist the associated producer as well? The answer is no! Persisting an entity does not perform the same operation on its associated entities as well, unless you customize what's called the cascade property.

The cascade property tells JPA which operations should be applied on associated entities when being performed on the owner entity. To enable this upon persisting a movie, the following property in the `@ManyToOne` annotation should be introduced:

```
@Entity
public class Movie {

    ...
    @ManyToOne(cascade=CascadeType.PERSIST)
    private  Producer producer;
    ...
}
```

Now, when trying to perform the persist operation on the movie entity, the same operation will be applied to the `producer` entity as well. You can specify many cascade types in the same annotation, for example:

```
@Entity
public class Movie {

    ...
    @ManyToOne(cascade={ CascadeType.PERSIST, CascadeType.REMOVE })
    private  Producer producer;
    ...
}
```

Now, when trying to persist or remove a movie, the same operation will be applied to the associated producer. This is not always the correct choice in fact, and in this case deleting a movie does not mean we should delete the associated producer, as the producer may be engaged in other movies. Therefore, a choice of which cascading operations to be applied should be considered carefully; thus, there is no cascading operation by default.

Now, let's explore a list of all available cascade property values:

CascadeType	Purpose
PERSIST	Persist the associated entities upon persisting the owner.
MERGE	Merge the associated entities upon merging the owner.
REMOVE	Remove the associated entities upon removing the owner.
REFRESH	Refresh the associated entities upon refreshing the owner.
DETACH	Detach the associated entities upon detaching the owner.
ALL	Cascade all operations, shorthand for specifying an array for all of the previous values.

Map collections of primitives

Sometimes, you need to associate your entity with a collection of primitive values to represent a simple one/many-to-many relationship. For example, each movie has a set of associated genres that we want to keep stored in the database. To represent them from an object-oriented perspective, we will define a list (collection) of strings in our Movie class. To reflect this relationship inside the database, we will use the @ElementCollecion annotation, as shown in the following example:

```
@Entity
public class Movie {

    @Id
    @GeneratedValue
    private long id;
    private String title;
    @ElementCollection
    private List<String> genres = new ArrayList<>();

    public Movie() {
    }
    // getters and setters here
}
```

The @ElementCollection annotation will make the JPA provider create another table (movie_genres) to store the list of genres, mapped to the movies table using the movie's primary key as a secondary key in the (movie_genres) table. Now, let's create a movie, associate some genres, then store it in the database:

```
Movie movie = new Movie();
movie.setTitle("Beauty and the Beast");
movie.getGenres().add("Family");
movie.getGenres().add("Fantasy");
movie.getGenres().add("Musicial");
movie.getGenres().add("Romance");
```

Referring to the database, you will find a movie_genres table has been created, with a list of the genres we have associated.

There are times when you will be required to customize the table name, and/or the foreign key used to map each genre to its owner movie. To do this, we can provide some attributes to the @ElementCollection annotation, as in the following example:

```
@Entity
public class Movie {

    @Id
    @GeneratedValue
    private long id;
    private String title;
    @CollectionTable(name = "movie_genres",
            joinColumns =@JoinColumn(name = "movie_title",
            referencedColumnName = "title"))
    @ElementCollection
    private List<String> genres = new ArrayList<>();

    public Movie() {
    }
    // getters and setters here
}
```

As you see, the name attribute is used to specify the secondary table's desired name. Moreover, the joinColumns annotation is used to specify which column will be used to join rows in the secondary table (with genres) to the primary one (with movies). We have provided an annotation (@JoinColumn) specifying two attributes: the name, which represents the join column name in the secondary table, and the referencedColumnName, which represents the name of the owner entity's attribute that will be used to map it. In this example, we have used the title, rather than the ID, as a mapping value for the secondary table.

JPA query language

The persistence query language (QL) is one of the most important parts of the Java Persistence API. As the name suggest, the JPA QL is used to perform complex queries on database entities and to perform bulk update operations. The JPA QL seems very similar to SQL. Actually, it borrows the same syntax, with one key difference: the JPA QL uses an object-oriented approach rather than a relational approach.

To use JPA queries, you will have first to instantiate a `query` object that you can use to execute queries using the JPA QL. Let's see an examples:

```
Query query = entityManager.createQuery("SELECT m FROM Movie m");
List<Query> results = query.getResultList();
```

As you can see, we have used the `createQuery` method of the `enitityManager` object to create a `query` object. We have passed a String containing the query itself as a parameter to this method. For sure, this query retrieves a list of all the movie entities that exist in the database.

In the second line, we have invoked the `getResultList` method to retrieve a list of the `query` objects. The method is used to execute the query and retrieve a list of all the results.

The syntax rules of the JPA QL will be discussed in detail in the following sections.

Basic syntax

As mentioned earlier, the syntax of the JPA QL is very similar to SQL. In fact, your knowledge of SQL will almost be enough to start using the JPA QL. However, there is an important rule of thumb that you should learn to be able to map your SQL knowledge to JPA QL successfully. The rule is that JPA QL is object-oriented, not relational!

What does this mean? This means that you are querying for objects (entities), not rows. You will use the entity name, not the table name. Moreover, you will assign named variables to objects, then you will use this name to supply the query with your clauses and/or your goals.

To get into this rule, let's start analyzing our first JPA QL statement mentioned in the previous example. The statement was:

```
SELECT x FROM Movie x
```

To understand the previous statement, let's read it from the second half:

```
FROM Movie x
```

This part tells the persistence provider to select all entities from the `Movie` table, naming each entity with the variable x. Then, here's the first half:

```
SELECT x
```

This means that you want to fetch all of them! To make this more obvious, let's append a clause to our statement:

```
SELECT x FROM Movie x WHERE x.title=:title
```

Now, the statement means that we wish to fetch all movies with a specific title. We have used the named variable x, with a period (.) followed by an attribute name, to denote that we target a specific value of the attribute. Now, the usage of the x variable has became clearer. But, what is this expression (`:title`), followed by the equals (=) sign ? This is called a named parameter, which will be the topic of the next section.

Query parameters

In the following sections, we are going to learn how to pass runtime values to our query in the Java Persistence API. It's very important to avoid other techniques of passing runtime parameters, such as string concatenation, as this way your application will be most probably infected with SQL injection leaks (actually PQL, not SQL).

Named parameters

Like in JDBC's prepared statement, JPA queries can include named parameters that can be replaced by inputs from the user, as in the following example:

```
Query query = entityManager.createQuery("SELECT m FROM Movie m WHERE
m.title=:title");
query.setParameter("title", "Beauty and the Beast");
Movie movie = (Movie) query.getSingleResult();
```

In this example, we have used the named parameter feature of JPA queries by including a parameter name of our choice prefixed with a colon (`:title`). Then, we have passed the desired value to this parameter by using the `setParameter` method of the `query` object. We can then use the query by executing the `getSingleResult` method, which will fetch a single result from the database.

Positional parameters

Query parameters can be used by using what's called positional parameters. A positional parameter is a number prefixed by a question mark (?), as in the following example:

```
Query query = entityManager.createQuery("SELECT m FROM Movie m WHERE
m.title=?1");
query.setParameter(1, "Beauty and the Beast");
Movie movie = (Movie) query.getSingleResult();
```

As you see, we have provided an integer denoting the index of the question mark to replace, rather than named parameters, as shown in the previous section.

 Note that positional parameters are one-based.

Query examples

In this section, we are going to learn the most common operations that we will need to perform in most enterprise applications. More complex use cases are supported too; you can refer to the JPA documentation to find out more about them.

Selecting entities

Retrieve all movie entities:

```
SELECT m FROM Movie m
```

Ordering entities

Retrieve all movie entities, ordering them by their title:

```
SELECT m FROM Movie m ORDER BY m.title
```

Limiting records

Retrieve all movie entities, ordering them by their title, but limiting the results to 10 only, starting from the first one. This is useful in pagination scenarios:

```
Query q = entityManager.createQuery("SELECT m FROM Movie m ORDER BY
m.title");
List<Movie> results =
q.setFirstResult(0).setMaxResults(10).getResultList();
```

Selecting entities with clauses

Retrieve all movie entities where title equals some specified value. You saw in the named parameters section how to pass this value.

```
SELECT m FROM Movie m WHERE m.title=:title
```

Selecting entities with projection

Retrieve all movie titles where the title is a specified value.

```
SELECT m.title FROM Movie m WHERE m.title LIKE :title
```

Eliminating duplicates

Retrieve all movie titles without duplicates.

```
SELECT DISTINCT m.title FROM Movie m
```

Entity navigation

Retrieve all `movie` entities where the `producer` name equals a specified value.

```
SELECT m FROM Movie m WHERE m.producer.name=:proucerName
```

Update entities

Update the status of a movie entity with a new one using a specified `id`.

```
UPDATE Movie m
SET m.status = :newStatus
WHERE m.id=:movieId
```

DELETE entities

Delete all entities with a specified status.

```
DELETE
FROM Movie m
WHERE m.status = :status
```

Using native SQL queries

In addition to the JPQL, you still can use native SQL queries within the JPA framework. There will be many cases where you cannot achieve your goal using the JPQL, especially when you are required to use some DBMS-specific syntax, or when you are to perform very complex queries that you cannot perform using the built-in JPQL.

In the following code, we are going to show how to perform native queries using JPA APIs:

```
Query q = entityManager.createNativeQuery("SELECT m.title, m.producer FROM
Movie m");
List<Object[]> movies = q.getResultList();

for (Object[] arr : movies) {
    System.out.println("(Movie) title:" + arr[0] +
                        ", producer:" + ((Producer) arr[1]).getName());
}
```

As you see, we have used the `createNativeQuery` method to create our native query. We later executed it using `getResultList` as we earlier did using JPA queries. But, as you can see, the result set is a list of array objects. That's because the entity manager is not aware of the type of results you are going to fetch. Therefore, each single result is represented using an array of objects, and each element of that array represents a single projection in the result fetched.

However, you can provide an additional parameter to the `createNativeQuery` method, specifying the type of instance you are going to fetch. This way, the entity manager will wrap the results into instances of the type you specified, as shown in the following example:

```
Query q = entityManager.createNativeQuery("SELECT m.title, m.producer FROM Movie m", Movie.class);
List<Movie> movies = q.getResultList();

for (Movie movie : movies) {
    System.out.println("(Movie) title:" + movie.getTitle()
                        + ", producer:" +
movie.getProducer().getName());
}
```

Named queries

A named query in JPA, as the name suggest, is a query you define and associate with your entities, which are given unique names, that can be used later to create the query without re-specifying its syntax. This way, you can remove the same query multiple times, without having to write it again.

To define a named query, we will annotate our entity with the `@NamedQuery` annotation, specifying the name and the query itself, as shown in the following example:

```
@Entity
@NamedQuery(name = "fetchAllMovies", query = "SELECT m FROM Movie m")
public class Movie {
....
}
```

Then, in order to use this query, we will use the `createNamedQuery` method, passing the name of our query, as shown in the following example:

```
Query q = entityManager.createNamedQuery("fetchAllMovies");
List<Movie> movies = q.getResultList();
```

Of course, we can specify queries with named parameters, as shown in the following example:

```
@Entity
@NamedQuery(name = "fetchMovie", query = "SELECT m FROM Movie m
WHERE m.id=:id")
```

```
public class Movie {
....
}
```

Then, we can create the query, pass the parameters, and execute it, as shown in the following example:

```
Query q = entityManager.createNamedQuery("fetchMovie");
q.setParameter("id", 101);
Movie movie = q.getSingleResult();
```

Criteria queries

Criteria queries are queries that can be built by instantiating Java objects, rather than specifying a string syntax. The advantage of this is that you can avoid query syntax errors; as the correctness of your queries will be guaranteed by the compiler, you can then detect syntax errors early.

The criteria query API may appear complex at first sight, but later you will get used to its syntax and use it without any hassle. Now, let's start examining a simple example to create a query equivalent to `SELECT x FROM Movie x` using the criteria API:

```
CriteriaBuilder cb = entityManager.getCriteriaBuilder(); //01
CriteriaQuery<Movie> q = cb.createQuery(Movie.class); //02
Root<Movie> root = q.from(Movie.class); //03
q.select(root); //04
List<Movie> movies = entityManager.createQuery(q).getResultList(); //05
```

Let's look though the previous example:

- In line 01, we have instantiated a criteria builder object; the criteria builder, as the name suggests, is an object that we will use to create a criteria query
- In line 02, we have used the criteria builder to create a criteria `query` object of type `Movie`
- In line 03, we have specified the entity (table) we will be selecting our results from (equivalent to `FROM Movie x`)
- In line 04, we have specified that we are going to select the `root` object itself (equivalent to `SELECT x`)
- In line 05, we have created a query using the criteria query we just created, then executed it using the `getResultList` method

Let's look through another example, which will be equavalent to SELECT x FROM Movie x WHERE x.id = 1:

```
CriteriaBuilder cb = entityManager.getCriteriaBuilder(); //01
CriteriaQuery<Movie> q =
entityManager.getCriteriaBuilder().createQuery(Movie.class); //02
Root<Movie> root = q.from(Movie.class); //03
q.select(root); //04
q.where(cb.equal(root.get("id"), 1)); //05
Movie movie = entityManager.createQuery(q).getSingleResult(); //06
```

The previous example is exactly like the earlier one, but adding the where clause in line 5. We have used the where method of the query object to express the where clause, passing the clause content. The clause content is created using the criteria builder object's equal method, which instantiates an object representing the equal clause, passing two parameters: the first one is the id attribute, which is obtained by executing the get method of the root object, which will be equivalent to x.id, and the second one is the value to test equality with. Therefore, we have created the x.id=1 clause.

For more details about the criteria API, please refer to the JPA 2.1 specification online.

Mapping inheritance

There are times when it will be very useful for entities to inherit from each others. Suppose, for example, that two entities Actor and Director exist, and each has a set of common attributes (name and birth date), but each has other specific attributes. It's very natural to create a Person superclass for them, putting inside it all the common attributes, then make both the Actor and Director inherit from it.

The question is, if we have used the mentioned design, how will our entities be mapped to the database ? In JPA, there are three **inheritance strategies** that can be used to achieve inheritance mapping:

- Single table strategy
- Joined table strategy
- Table per class strategy

In the following sections, we are going to look at each strategy in detail.

Single table strategy

In the single table strategy, only one table will be used to represent all entities in the inheritance relationship. All common attributes, as well as the specific attributes, will be used as columns in one table. As we will see in the next example, two entities are introduced (Actor and Director), with one common superclass (Person). If we have persisted either an instance of Actor or an instance of Person, both will be stored in the same table. But the question is, How will JPA later differentiate between the two instances inside this table? And one more question, What about the specific attributes of actors, when storing an instance of a director?

The answer to the first question is that JPA uses a discriminator column. The discriminator column is used to specify, for each row, which instance type is stored inside this row. It means that for each actor, a discrimination value (for example, actor) will be used in a special column to specify that this row holds an actor, not a director.

The answer to the second question is that JPA uses null values for columns that are specific to other entities. For example, in an actor row, the director's specific columns will be null, and vice versa.

Now, let's implement a single table strategy example. We will define three classes (Person, Actor, and Director) with the required attributes and specifying the inheritance relationship, then apply some annotations.

The @Inheritance annotation is used on the superclass entity, passing the strategy value as a single table. The @Inheritance annotation will be used in all strategies, as will be shown later. The @DiscriminatorColumn annotation will be used on the superclass in the single table strategy to specify the name of the special column that will exist to differentiate between the different types of entities. The @DiscriminatorValue annotation will be used in each subclass to specify a discrimination value for each entity. Let's see an example of this all:

```
@Entity
@Inheritance(strategy = InheritanceType.SINGLE_TABLE)
@DiscriminatorColumn(name = "type")
public class Person {

    @Id
    @GeneratedValue
    private long id;
    private String name;
    @Temporal(TemporalType.DATE)
    private Date birthDate;
```

```
    public Person() {
    }

    // getters and setters here
}

@Entity
@DiscriminatorValue(value = "ACTOR")
public class Actor extends Person        {

    private String biography;

    public Actor() {
    }

    // getters and setters here
}

@Entity
@DiscriminatorValue(value = "DIRECTOR")
public class Director extends Person {

    private String dir;

    public Director() {
}

    // getters and setters here
}
```

Now, let's persist an instance of `Actor`:

```
SimpleDateFormat sdf = new SimpleDateFormat("MM/dd/yyyy");

Actor actor = new Actor();
actor.setName("Emma Watson");
actor.setBiography("Born in Paris, France.");
actor.setBirthDate(sdf.parse("04/15/1990"));
entityManager.persist(actor);
```

Then, let's persist an instance of `Director`:

```
Director director = new Director();
director.setName("Bill Condon");
director.setBirthDate(sdf.parse("10/22/1955"));
director.setDir("Born in New York.");
entityManager.persist(director);
```

The resulting table will look like the following:

ID	type	BIRTHDATE	NAME	DIR	BIOGRAPHY
1	ACTOR	1990-04-15	Emma Watson	NULL	....
2	DIRECTOR	1955-10-22	Bill Condon	....	NULL

Joined table strategy

In the joined table strategy, a table for each class in our relationship will exist in the database. In our example, three tables will exist (`Person`, `Actor`, and `Director`). The `Person` table will include the common columns found in the person entity. Both the actor and director tables will includes specific columns for each of them. When persisting an actor, for example, a row will be inserted in the person table, with the attributes inherited from the person, and another one will be inserted in the actor table, with the specific attributes for that actor. A discriminator column will be used in the `Person` table, as shown in the previous strategy, which we will ignore in this example and retain their defaults. Now, let's see an example of this:

```
@Entity
@Inheritance(strategy = InheritanceType.JOINED)
public class Person {
    ....
}

@Entity
@PrimaryKeyJoinColumn(referencedColumnName = "id")
public class Actor extends Person {
    ....
}

@Entity
@PrimaryKeyJoinColumn(referencedColumnName="id")
public class Director extends Person {
    ....
}
```

After performing the persistence operations shown in the previous section, the resulting table will look like the following:

Person

ID	DTYPE	type	BIRTHDATE	NAME
1	Actor	ACTOR	1990-04-15	Emma Watson
2	Director	DIRECTOR	1955-10-22	Bill Condon

Actor

ID	BIOGRAPHY
1	....

Director

ID	DIR
2	....

Table per class strategy

In the table per class strategy, there will be a separate table for each concrete class. In our example, there will be a separate table for Person and a separate table for Actor, with all the attributes even inherited from the superclass Actor, and the same applies to the director class:

```
@Entity
@Inheritance(strategy = InheritanceType.TABLE_PER_CLASS)
public class Person {
    ....
}

@Entity
public class Actor extends Person {
    ....
}

@Entity
public class Director extends Person {
    ....
}
```

After performing the same persistence operations shown in the previous section, the resulting table will look like the following:

Person

ID	type	BIRTHDATE	NAME

Actor

ID	type	BIRTHDATE	NAME	BIOGRAPHY
1	ACTOR	1990-04-15	Emma Watson	....

Director

ID	type	BIRTHDATE	NAME	DIR
2	DIRECTOR	1955-10-22	Bill Condon	....

Comparing strategies

In the following table, we are going to explore the different advantages and disadvantages related to each of the previous strategies:

Strategy	Advantages	Disadvantages
Single-table	- Good query performance - Only one table is used, so no extra tables are required	- Cannot include nullable attributes in subclasses
Joined	- No redundant columns exist in database tables	- Poor query performance as joins are required
Table per class	- Good query performance when querying for subclasses	- Poor query performance when querying for root classes, as it requires multiple queries in subclass tables - Ordering issues when querying for roots, as data exists in multiple tables, and hence JPA orders by class

Polymorphic queries

One of the great features of JPA inheritance mapping is that you can perform polymorphic queries on your entities. By polymorphic queries, we mean that we can query for a `root` class, where the resulting list includes instances of the different subclasses that match the query parameters we specified. For example, we can query for a person by name, where the results list may include both actors and directors that match the name criteria we have specified.

Let's look though this feature using the following example:

```
Query query = entityManager.createQuery("SELECT x FROM Person x WHERE
x.name like :name");
query.setParameter("name", "John%");
List<Person> results = query.getResultList();

for (Person result : results) {
    if (result instanceof Actor) {
        Actor actor = (Actor) result;
        System.out.println("An acotr found with name " +
actor.getName());
    } else if (result instanceof Director) {
        Director director = (Director) result;
        System.out.println("A director found with name " +
director.getName());
    }
}
```

In the previous example, we have created a query to search for persons by name, then we executed the query, fetching a list of the available results. The returned list will be a collection of both actors and directors that meet the specified criteria. In our loop, we have used the instanceof Java operator to differentiate between actor and director results, as the actual instances behind our persons list will be either actors or directors.

Moreover, we can specify the type of the desired objects in the where clause itself. For example, if we need to look for only directors, we can use the following query:

```
SELECT x FROM Person x WHERE x.name like :name AND type(x)=Director
```

For sure, it makes no sense to use only one type in our query, as it would be more logical to query for directors directly. However, supposing we have extended our example to include more subclass types rather than only actors and directors; using a combination of two or more would then makes sense, as in the following example:

```
SELECT x FROM Person x WHERE x.name like :name AND type(x) in (Actor,
Director)
```

Summary

In this chapter, we learned how to use the Java Persistence APIs to do database-related operations using object-oriented approaches. This is really going to simplify your data access layer in your application, as the efforts of mapping objects to relational things will be avoided, freeing you to focus on your business logic.

And now, it's time to keep our data consistent by stopping any incorrect business data from getting passed to our data objects using the Bean Validation API 2.0, which will be our topic in the next chapter. Get ready!

4
Validating Data with Bean Validation 2.0

Validating data is one of the most common and important operations in an enterprise solution. Whatever your application domain is, you should always validate your data against the proposed business constraints, and in the different layers of your application. You should always validate data entered directly by the user (in the presentation layer), data received by your web services, data received by your business objects, and data before being sent to the database (in the data access layer).

But why you should validate your data in all application layers rather than the presentation layer, which has direct contact with your end user?

The answer is this: you may expose a web service layer to allow integration with third parties, or even have a set of web services to support your frontend without an intent to expose them to third parties, and still a hacker can find a way to call your services in a way that violates your business constraints. This is one of the most common ways a hacker has to find a malicious way into your system.

You or some other developers may misuse your APIs, or a bug can occur in such a way that invalid parameters may be sent to different beans and methods, which will lead to corruption in the application state. The problem is that rewriting the validation logic everywhere will result in a big mess, and of course break your application's maintainability.

Therefore, the bean validation API is provided with Java EE, with the slogan: *Annotate once, validate everywhere*. Although it's a very simple API, it plays a very critical and important role in your enterprise middleware solutions, which we are going to discuss in this chapter.

In following sections, we are going to learn about:

- Performing programmatic and automatic bean validations
- Validating graphs of objects in a bean
- Different validation constraints available
- Validating bean method parameters and return values
- Defining custom validation constraints

What's new in Bean Validation 2.0?

If you are already familiar with the bean validation API up to version 1.1, bean validation 2.0 comes with a set of new features that increases its maturity and compatibility with Java 8, and provides the missing features that were always requested and needed by Java developers. The bean validation specification states the following about the changes made in version 2.0:

> *"The main contribution of Bean Validation 2.0 is leveraging the new language features and API additions of Java 8 for the purposes of validation. Java 8 or later is required to use Bean Validation 2.0."*

Some of the interesting changes include:

- New built-in constraints such as `@Email`, `@NotEmpty`, `@NotBlank`, `@Positive`, `@PositiveOrZero`, `@Negative`, `@NegativeOrZero`, `@PastOrPresent` and `@FutureOrPresent`, which make it more usable
- Support for new date/time data types such as `@Past` and `@Future`
- Support for using repeatable annotations, introduced in Java 8, which makes its configuration much simpler

 You can refer to the documentation for a full list of changes made in version 2.0.

First validation example

In the following example, we are going to show how to use the bean validation API to validate our application beans against a set of constraints. Recalling our `Movie` entity, we are going to force the user to give each movie title a value, banning him/her from letting it be a null value. This makes sense, as of course there will never be a movie with no title at all. Let's see how we can do this with the bean validation API.

Well, in fact, it's too simple. We will just annotate the title field with the `@NotNull` annotation, part of a set of built-in constraints provided with the bean validation API, as shown in the following example:

```
@Entity
public class Movie {
    ....
    @NotNull
    private String title;
    ....
}
```

`@NotNull` is used to check whether the variable has a value or not; if the variable has a value, then the bean is considered to be in a valid state. Otherwise, if it's null, the bean is considered to be in an invalid state.

But how and when will bean values be checked against their associated constraints? There are mainly two approaches to validating our application beans:

- Programmatic validation
- The framework's built-in integration with the bean validation API

By the first approach, we mean that we will be performing the validation problematically using some classes and interfaces provided by the bean validation API. However, it's more common to depend on the second approach. Many Java frameworks have built-in integration with the bean validation API, so they will perform the desired validation when needed. For example, the Java persistence API will validate your beans against specified constraints automatically upon trying to persist new entities, or to commit some changes to an existing one.

First approach – programmatic validation

Let's examine the first approach and try to validate our bean pragmatically. The bean validation API provides the Validator interface, which exposes a set of methods used to validate our beans. In order to obtain an instance of the default implementation of the Validator interface, we will use the Validation class, which is also a part of the bean validation API. With buildDefaultValidatorFactory(), we will build a ValidatorFactory object, which will be used to build the object that implements the Validator interface, as shown in the following code snippet:

```
ValidatorFactory validatorFactory =
Validation.buildDefaultValidatorFactory();
Validator validator = validatorFactory.getValidator();

Movie untitledMovie = new Movie();
Set<ConstraintViolation<Movie>> violations =
validator.validate(untitledMovie);

for (ConstraintViolation<Movie> violation : violations) {
    System.out.println(violation.getPropertyPath());
    System.out.println(violation.getMessage());
}
```

In the previous code, we have created a validator object in the first two lines of code, as explained earlier. We have also created an instance of the Movie class, called untitledMovie, without specifying any value for the title attribute. Therefore, the title attribute will have the default value, null. We have passed the object to the validate() method of the validator object. The method returns a set instance of ConstraintViolation implementations. As the name suggests, each ConstraintViolation includes a constraint violation found in the specified bean, alongside all the details about such a violation, such as the property that includes the violation and the error message associated with this violation.

If all the bean attributes are valid, then the returned set will be empty. Otherwise, as in our example, the returned set will include all the found violations in our beans. As you can see in the previous example, we have performed a for each loop over the constraint violations, printing each violation's propertyPath and associated message.

Running the previous example, the output will be:

```
title
cannot be null
```

But what if we need to customize the violation message associated with our constraint `violation` objects? We can customize those messages by setting the message attribute of the constraint annotation to whatever message you like, as follows:

```
@Entity
public class Movie {

    ....
            @NotNull(message = "Title cannot be null")
    private String title;
    ....
}
```

Running the previous example, the output will be:

```
title
Title cannot be null
```

As you see, calling the `getMessage()` method returns our newly specified message.

Second approach – auto validation

Now, let's move on to the second approach, which is delegating the bean validation to other frameworks integrated with the bean validation API. One of those APIs is the Java Persistence API; it performs bean validation automatically upon trying to persist new, or commit changes to exist, entities.

Recalling what we have learned in the previous chapter, we will be trying to persist a `movie` object with a null title, as follows:

```
@Transactional
@RequestScoped
public class MovieBean {

    @PersistenceContext(name = "jpa-examplesPU")
    private EntityManager entityManager;

    public void createNewMovie() {

        Movie movie = new Movie();
        entityManager.persist(movie);
    }
}
```

Running the previous example, the output will be:

```
javax.validation.ConstraintViolationException: Bean Validation
constraint(s) violated while executing Automatic Bean Validation on
callback event:'prePersist'. Please refer to embedded ConstraintViolations
for details.
```

As you see, the JPA framework has thrown a validation exception upon trying to persist an entity with an invalid state. The JPA framework, alongside many other frameworks in Java, performs bean validation on your entities before using them. This type of integration with the bean validation API makes you define your constraint only once; then, it will be applied in all different contexts across your application layers and components.

Injecting the validator object

Recalling the first approach, and rather than programmatically creating the `validator` object by creating a `ValidatorFactory` using the `Validation` class and so on, you can simply inject the `Validator` object as a dependency using the CDI, as shown in the following example:

```
@RequestScoped
public class MovieBean {

    @PersistenceContext(name = "jpa-examplesPU")
    private EntityManager entityManager;
    @Inject
    private Validator validator;

    public void validateMovie() {

        Movie movie = new Movie();

        Set<ConstraintViolation<Movie>> violations =
validator.validate(movie);
        for (ConstraintViolation<Movie> violation : violations) {
            System.out.println(violation.getPropertyPath());
            System.out.println(violation.getMessage());
        }
    }
}
```

As you see, the `validator` object is injected as a dependency rather than having to create it with many lines of code. There will be cases when you need to perform programmatic validation, although this will be rare. Anyway, whenever you need to perform programmatic validation, you can simply inject the `Validator` object using the `@Inject` annotation.

Graph validation

The bean validation API also supports graph validation, which means that if some object is referencing another one, you can define a constraint that your embedded object should also be validated from the owner's one context, according to the constraints defined in the embedded object.

Let's try this with an example; we will define a `Producer` class with a constraint on the name attribute as follows:

```
public class Producer {

    @NotNull
    private String name;

    // setters and getters here

}
```

Then, we will modify our `Movie` object so it references an instance of the `Producer` object, as follows:

```
public class Movie {

    @NotNull
    private String title;
    @Valid
    private Producer producer;

    public Movie() {
    }
    // setters and getters here
}
```

Note the `@Valid` attribute; it tells the bean validator that when validating the `Movie` object, the `Producer` object should also be validated.

Now, let's try to create a movie and producer objects with null values, make the movie reference the producer, then try to validate it programmatically as shown in the earlier example:

```
Movie movie = new Movie();
movie.setProducer(new Producer());
// validation code mentioned earlier
```

The output of the previous code should be:

```
title
may not be null
producer.name
may not be null
```

As you can see, the bean validator could detect a null title in the `movie` object, in addition to a null name in the referenced `producer` object.

Moreover, the bean validation API is able to validate an array or list of objects. For example, recalling the `Movie-Actor` relationship, we can let the bean validation API validate a list of actors associated with a movie instance, as shown in the following example:

```
public class Actor {

    @NotNull
    private String name;

    // setters and getters here

}

public class Movie {

    @NotNull
    private String title;
    @Valid
    private List<Actor> actors;

    public Movie() {
    }
    // setters and getters here
}

Movie movie = new Movie();
movie.getActors().add(new Actor());
movie.getActors().add(new Actor());
// validation code mentioned earlier
```

Run the previous example and the output should be:

```
actors[0].name
may not be null
title
may not be null
actors[1].name
may not be null
```

As you see, the bean validation API was able to detect constraint violations on the list of actors, denoting each one by its index.

List of available constraints

In the following table, we are going to list all available built-in constraints in the bean validation 2.0 APIs, with explanations and examples. For more detailed information, you can check the complete bean validation 2.0 API docs:

Constraint	Explanation
@AssertFalse/AssertTrue	• Checks whether the annotated element's value is false/true, respectively. • The annotated element type might either be boolean (primitive) or Boolean (a primitive wrapper instance).
@DecimalMax/DecimalMin	• Checks the value of the annotated element to see whether it's a number whose value must be lower than or equal to the specified maximum (for DecimalMax), or higher than or equal to the specified minimum (for DecimalMin). • Supported types are: BigDecimal, BigInteger, String, and byte, short, int, long, and their respective wrappers. • Example: @DecimalMax("12.25")
@Digits	• Checks the annotated element's value is a number within the accepted range • The integer attribute used to specify the number of digits that should be found in the integral part, where the fraction attribute is used to specify the number of digits that should be found in the fractional part • Supported types are: BigDecimal, BigInteger, String, and byte, short, int, long, and their respective wrappers • Example: @Digits(integer = 4,fraction = 2)

@Future/@Past	• Checks the value of the annotated element to see if it's an instance of a date or time in the future (for @Future), or in the past (for @Past) • Null elements are considered valid • Supported types are: Date, Calendar, Instant, LocalDate, LocalDateTime, LocalTime, MonthDay, OffsetDateTime, OffsetTime, Year, YearMonth, ZonedDateTime, HijrahDate, JapaneseDate, MinguoDate, and ThaiBuddhistDate
@Max/@Min	• Checks the value of the annotated element to see if it's a number whose value is lower than or equal to the specified maximum (for @Max), or is higher than or equal to the specified minimum (for @Min) • Supported types are: BigDecimal BigInteger, and byte, short, int, long, and their respective wrappers • null elements are considered valid
@NotNull	• Checks the value of the annotated element is not null • Accepts any type
@Pattern	• Checks that the value of the annotated CharSequence matches a specified regular expression. The regular expression follows Java regular expression conventions • null elements are considered valid

@Size	• Checks the size of the value of the annotated element is between specified boundaries
	• Min and Max attributes are used to specify this boundary
	• Min value can be specified without a max; max will be assigned the default value of 2147483647
	• Max value can be specified without min; min will be assigned the default value of zero
	• Supported types are:
	  ○ CharSequence (length of character sequence is evaluated)
	  ○ Collection (collection size is evaluated)
	  ○ Map (map size is evaluated)
	  ○ Array (array length is evaluated)
	• null elements are considered valid.
	• Example: @Size(min= 2, max = 255)

@FutureOrPresent	• Checks the value of the annotated element if it's a string of a well-formed email address. • Exact semantics of what makes up a valid email address are left to bean validation providers. • Accepts CharSequence.

@NotEmpty	• Checks the value of the annotated element must not be null or empty
	• Supported types are:
	  ○ CharSequence (length of character sequence is evaluated)
	  ○ Collection (collection size is evaluated)
	  ○ Map (map size is evaluated)
	  ○ Array (array length is evaluated)

@Positive/@Negative	• Checks the value of the annotated element; it must be a strictly positive number (0 is considered an invalid value) in the case of @Positive, or a strictly negative number in the case of @Negative • Supported types are: BigDecimal, BigInteger, and byte, short, int, long, float, double and their respective wrappers • null elements are considered valid

Validating parameters and return values

With the bean validation API, you can also validate your method parameters and return values. By validating the method parameters, you can ensure that the business preconditions that should be met have been met, before calling your business code (for example, never withdraw a negative value!), whereas, by validating method return values, you can guarantee the postconditions that should be met after executing your business code (for example, never return a negative value for a calculated outstanding balance!).

To validate a method parameter, just annotate the parameter with the appropriate constraint, as in the following code:

```
@RequestScoped
public class MovieBean {

    public void createMovie(@NotNull String title) {
        // do some actions here
    }
}

// from another bean
movieBean.createMovie (null);
```

By trying to call the createMovie() method and passing a null parameter, as shown in the previous example, a validation exception will be thrown, indicating that the preconditions you specified could not be met.

To validate method return values, just annotate your method with the constraint you want, as shown in the following example:

```
@RequestScoped
public class MovieBean {

    @NotNull
     public Movie createMovie(@NotNull String something) {
            // do some actions here
            return null;
    }
}

// from another bean
Movie r = movieBean.createMovies("text");
```

By trying to call the `createMovie()` method, the null value returned from inside it will cause a validation exception to be thrown, indicating that the postcondition you have specified could not be met.

Defining a custom constraint

With the bean validation API, you can also introduce custom constraints, rather than the built-in ones, in order to reuse more complex validation logic in different contexts within your application. This is one of the best features and introduces a great flexibility and reusability in real-world validation scenarios.

Let's introduce a custom constraint, called `CheckCase`, which is used to check whether a string is uppercase or lowercase, according to the developer's preference. The constraint will include a type attribute, which will be given either the value of UPPER or LOWER. If the type attribute was given the UPPER value, then it will check the given string to see if it's in uppercase or not. Otherwise, if it was given the LOWER value, then it will check if the given string is in lowercase or not.

To define this custom constraint, we will perform two key steps:

1. Creating a constraint annotation.
2. Creating a validator class associated with this annotation.

Let's perform our first step and create the constraint annotation. Create an annotation, called `CheckCase`, with the following code:

```
@Documented
@Target({ElementType.FIELD, ElementType.METHOD, ElementType.PARAMETER})
@Retention(RUNTIME)
@Constraint(validatedBy = CheckCaseValidator.class)
public @interface CheckCase {

    String message() default "invalid string case!";
    Class<?>[] groups() default {};
    Class<? extends Payload>[] payload() default {};
    CaseType type() default CaseType.UPPER;

    public static enum CaseType {
        UPPER, LOWER
    }
}
```

In the previous code, we have declared an annotation named `CheckCase`, with the following. Here is an explanation of the key parts of the annotation declaration:

- `@Target`: Tells the compiler that this annotation targets fields, methods, and parameters.
- `@Constraint`: This is the key annotation that tells the validation API that our annotation is a constrained one. The `validateBy` property is the most important one here, as it specifies the class that will perform the real validation action. This class's content will be discussed in the next section.
- Attribute message: Defines the message associated with violating this constraint; we have provided a default value denoting the default message if the user has not specified his/her own message.
- Attribute type: This is a custom attribute we have created to let the user choose the checking type, whether uppercase or lowercase. The type property is of the custom `enum CaseType`, which we have defined as an inner one in our annotation.
- Attribute groups: A mandatory attribute; its purpose of it is beyond this book.
- Attribute payload: A mandatory attribute; its purpose of it is is beyond this book.

Now, let's go on to our next step and create the constraint `validator` object. Create a class called `CheckCaseValidator`, implementing the `ConstraintValidator` interface, as shown in the following snippet:

```
public class CheckCaseValidator implements ConstraintValidator<CheckCase,
String> {

    private CheckCase.CaseType caseType;

    @Override
    public void initialize(CheckCase constraintAnnotation) {
        caseType = constraintAnnotation.type();
    }

    @Override
    public boolean isValid(String value, ConstraintValidatorContext
context) {
        if (value == null) {
            return true;
        } else if (caseType == CheckCase.CaseType.UPPER) {
            return value.equals(value.toUpperCase());
        } else {
            return value.equals(value.toLowerCase());
        }
    }

}
```

As you see, in the previous code we have implemented the `ConstraintValidator` interface, passing the following types to its generic parameters: `CheckCase` and `String`. The first one tells the validation API that this validator is associated to the `CheckCase` annotation. The second one tells the validation API that this validator is used on `String` values.

We have overridden its two abstract methods: initialize and `isValid`. The initialize method is used to perform any initialization operations needed by the `validator` object. The `isValid` method is used to perform the actual validation.

In our `CheckCaseValidator`, we have used the initialize method to pick the type property from the annotation object, which is passed to the initialize method. We remembered this property in a member variable, to be used later in the `validate()` method. In the `validate` method, we received the value and checked our `caseType`; if it's upper, then we check the string if it's upper, else, we have checked it if it's lower. One exception is when the string is null; we will consider a null value to be a valid one. By returning false from this method, we tell the bean validation API that the given value violates our constraint.

Now, let's use our custom constraint. We will annotate the title attribute in the `Movie` class with the `@CheckCase` annotation, setting the type to upper, as shown in the following example:

```
public class Movie {

    @CheckCase(type = CheckCase.CaseType.UPPER)
    private String title;

    // setters and getters here
}
```

Now, let's try to test our constraint. We will create a `Movie` instance, setting the title attribute to a small case string, then apply the programmatic validation code shown earlier as follows:

```
Movie movie = new Movie();
movie.setTitle("test");

Validator validator =
Validation.buildDefaultValidatorFactory().getValidator();
Set<ConstraintViolation<Movie>> violations = validator.validate(movie);
for (ConstraintViolation<Movie> violation : violations) {
    System.out.println(violation.getPropertyPath());
    System.out.println(violation.getMessage());
}
```

The output of the previous code should be:

```
title
invalid string case!
```

Associating messages with attributes

In the previous example, we have seen that upon constraint violation, our message is just returned to indicate what went wrong. However, the `invalid string case!` message was just not informative enough; we should include a more descriptive message to be returned with our `violation` object. We should tell the user whether the string should be upper or lower, according to the property the user has provided with the annotation property `type`. We can make the message include the expected case, as shown in the following example:

```
@Documented
@Constraint(validatedBy = CheckCaseValidator.class)
@Target({ElementType.ANNOTATION_TYPE, ElementType.CONSTRUCTOR,
ElementType.FIELD, ElementType.METHOD, ElementType.PARAMETER})
@Retention(RUNTIME)
public @interface CheckCase {
    String message() default "invalid string case, it should be in
{type}case!";
    . . . .
}
```

As you see, we have included the `{type}` expression inside the message. The curly braces are a special notation inside the message string denoting that we need to replace it with the `type` property originally set with the annotation. If you run the previous example, we will have the following output:

title
invalid string case, it should be in UPPERcase!

You may notice that UPPER is written in uppercase; that's because the default implementation of the `toString()` method of an `enum` object is the `enum` name itself. However, we can customize the word by overriding the `toString()` method and providing a neater form, as in the following example:

```
@Documented
@Constraint(validatedBy = CheckCaseValidator.class)
@Target({ElementType.ANNOTATION_TYPE, ElementType.CONSTRUCTOR,
ElementType.FIELD, ElementType.METHOD, ElementType.PARAMETER})
@Retention(RUNTIME)
public @interface CheckCase {

    String message() default "invalid string case, it should be in
{type}case!";
    . . . .
    public static enum CaseType {
```

```
UPPER {
    @Override
    public String toString() {
        return "upper";
    }
}, LOWER {
    @Override
    public String toString() {
        return "lower";
    }
}
    }
}
```

As you can see, we have overridden the `toString()` methods of both the UPPER and LOWER enum values, returning the words `"upper"` and `"lower"` respectively. If we run the previous example, we will have the following output:

title
invalid string case, it should be in uppercase!

Now, we have provided a neater form for the message to the user.

Adding more constraints

One of the extensibility features of the bean validation API is that you can associate your custom constraints with extra constraints. You can, for example, annotate the CheckCase constraint with one or more of the built-in constraints, as in the following examples:

```
@Documented
@Constraint(validatedBy = CheckCaseValidator.class)
@Target({ElementType.ANNOTATION_TYPE, ElementType.CONSTRUCTOR,
ElementType.FIELD, ElementType.METHOD, ElementType.PARAMETER})
@Retention(RUNTIME)
@Size(max=10)
public @interface CheckCase { .... }
```

As you see, in the previous code we have added the @Size annotation, with the max attribute set to 10, to the CheckCase constraint. The @Size annotation, as mentioned earlier, is a built-in constraint in the bean validation API, telling that bean validator that the string should be a max length of 10, as we specified.

Now, let's try to create a movie instance as follows:

```
Movie movie = new Movie();
movie.setTitle("tEST MORE THAN 10");
```

As you see, we have set the title to an invalid attribute, with a length exceeding 10, and with the invalid case at the same time. Now, let's validate our bean with the following code:

```
Validator validator =
Validation.buildDefaultValidatorFactory().getValidator();
Set<ConstraintViolation<Movie>> violations = validator.validate(movie);
for (ConstraintViolation<Movie> violation : violations) {
    System.out.println(violation.getPropertyPath());
    System.out.println(violation.getMessage());
}
```

The output will be:

```
title
size must be between 0 and 10
title
Invalid string case, it should be in uppercase!
```

Summary

In this chapter, we learned to use the bean validation API, and how to integrate it into our enterprise middleware solutions. There is more to learn about the bean validation API; you can refer to the specification for more details about its advanced topics. However, what we have learned in this chapter is enough to fulfill our day-to-day needs. The framework also has its own integration in frontend technologies such as JSP and JSF; however, the frontend is beyond the scope of this book.

In the next chapter, we will go through the Enterprise Java Beans technology, one of the most important specifications in Java EE 8.

Exposing Web Services with JAX-RS 2.1

In the era of cloud computing, web services are considered the key technology in making computer systems talk to each other and, more specifically, making application frontends talk to their backends, and sometimes to other third-party integrations. Whenever you share something to your favorite social media network, exchange messages with your friends, or pay for something online using your credit card, there is a web service, sitting far away in some computer in the cloud, being invoked upon your action!

In this chapter, we are going to cover the following topics:

- What are web services?
- Creating and calling RESTful services using JAX-RS
- Using Postman to test your RESTful services
- Accepting and processing user parameters
- Producing JSON responses
- Uploading files
- Server-sent events

What are web services?

Web services are functions that are deployed on one server and can be called remotely from any other system. Calling functions remotely is not something new, it was always a primary concept in building distributed systems. Dozens of methodologies and protocols were invented to support remote function calling—CORBA, IIOP, DCOM, and many other technologies are good examples of the idea. However, web services have gained popularity and domination over all of those, and we will soon show why.

The basic idea of web services is very simple, and can be summarized in three steps:

1. You write a function
2. You deploy the function on a web server
3. You assign the function a unique URL

For example, if you need to use a function that lists a set of products of another system, you may write this function, deploy it on some server, and give it the following URL: `http://example.com/products`.

If you open this URL in a web browser, you should see a list of all available products. It's very similar to browsing a web page, but the difference is that the web service should not display products in a fancy HTML page with attractive images and nice colors; it will display them in a specific text format. What format? That doesn't matter but it should be a format that another computer program can easily parse.

The key idea behind web services is that they reuse the HTTP protocol that was initially invented to deliver web pages to remote machines (or what we call machine-to-human interaction), to deliver formatted information to remote machines (or what we call machine-to-machine interaction). In other words, the same protocol used for web browsing is used in web services for remote function calls.

Back to the products example, the other system needs to consume this list of products and will call the mentioned URL, of course not using a web browser, but using a client-side API for HTTP manipulation. After receiving the formatted list of products, as a result, they will be parsed and the next action will be performed according to this result.

Well, in fact, and to be more technical, web services are not limited to the HTTP protocol. Other web protocols may be used to implement web services, such as SMTP for example. However, to be more realistic, HTTP has gained wider acceptance and become the de facto protocol for implementing web services. Therefore, and for the rest of this chapter, we will consider web services to be limited to the HTTP protocol in our technical clarifications.

The pros of web services over any other remote procedure call methodology are:

- Web services use purely standard web technologies that are supported by all programming languages and platforms
- Web services are programming language-agnostic; they offer the easiest and best integration mechanisms between systems of different programming languages

Web service use cases include:

- Web application frontends invoking system functionalities and rendering results as changes to the UI, which is known as the AJAX technique
- Mobile applications
- Integrating backends with each other

RESTful versus SOAP services

Web services are generally divided into two categories:

- RESTful services
- SOAP services

The difference between the two categories may appear confusing at first sight. However, we will try to clarify the differences.

SOAP services

SOAP is a standard communication protocol for exchanging structured messages between computer systems in the XML-based message format. It stands for Simple Object Access Protocol and defines a set of rules associated with messages being sent from one system to another, and a response message is received by this other system. Some key concepts are associated with SOAP services; **WSDL (Web Services Description Language)** is a standard way of defining a directory of SOAP-based services, message format, and other required information. Some

RESTful services

RESTful (Representational state transfer), on the other hand, is not another protocol for implementing web services. It's considered an architectural pattern for implementing web services. This means that RESTful does not define a message format for communication between a client and a server by itself; rather it defines a set of concepts to building web services, which can be implemented using any messaging format of your choice.

The key characteristic of RESTful services is that they are stateless. No transactional state is maintained between different functions; a call to one function, then restarting a server, and a call to another should always be guaranteed to return the same state. This tends to be natural with the HTTP protocol itself. SOAP, on the other hand, can sometimes be used in stateful contexts, where user data may be maintained using cookies or other methods.

Moreover, RESTful services don't have a built-in security model, although standard HTTP security mechanisms can be used with them. SOAP, on the other hand, has extended features for security.

Understanding all the differences is not easy at first, and may be confusing as mentioned earlier. However, by being involved in more scenarios and building web services, the picture will become clearer to you. Both SOAP and RESTful are powerful enough to satisfy all the needs for building web services based architecture, and both have proven themselves to fit all use scenarios. The choice between them depends on things such as organizational culture, legacy systems, types of other systems to integrate with, and so on. However, most newly created systems are built using RESTful architecture, especially for those with lightweight clients, such as mobile applications.

Anyways, the scope of this chapter is limited to RESTful web services, which we will discuss in detail in the upcoming sections.

Understanding HTTP

Before delving into RESTful services, a good awareness of the HTTP protocol is a key to understanding how to think and implement web services using the RESTful architectural style. If feel that you are good enough in HTTP, you can skip this section.

Basics

HTTP is a text-based request-response protocol. The basic idea of communicating between a client and a server using HTTP is as follows:

1. A Client (called user-agent) connects to the HTTP server
2. The user agent sends a request
3. Terver sends a response
4. The connection is terminated

The current version of HTTP most widely used is HTTP/1.1, but HTTP/2 has been around since 2015, it just has not gained wide implementation yet.

HTTP request

Suppose you have navigated using your web browser to the following URL: `http://example.com/products`.

The browser (user-agent) connects to the example.com server on port 80 (the default port for web servers), and sends its request. The request may contain many details, but we will examine an example of a minimum one that satisfies the server to make it understand what we need from it:

```
GET /products HTTP1.1            (request line)
Host: example.com        (header)
User-Agent: Firefox      (header)
```

The first line of the request is called the request line, and consists of the following:

- `GET`: The method used to perform our request; other methods are available (such as `POST`, `PUT`, and `DELETE`). `GET` means we request for a resource retrieval, whereas `POST`, for example, means we are sending data to a server, in some other scenarios.
- `/products`: The request path; this defines what resource we are requesting for retrieval from this server.
- `HTTP/1.1`: The protocol that we use in our request; this will always be written like this in all HTTP requests unless we are using another version.

The following lines of the HTTP request include what's called HTTP headers. Headers are metadata associated with our request and include a lot of useful information needed by the server. Headers are written in this format: (*HEADER-NAME: HEADER-VALUE*), as shown in the previous example. Not all headers are required by the server, but the host header is. The host header tells the web server which domain we are requesting, as a single web server may hosts two or more domains. The user-agent header is optional, but it's very useful for the web server to identify which client you use. The web server can identify which browser (Firefox or Chrome, for example), or device (desktop machine or tablet, for example) you are using to access the web page; this way, the server can respond with a page that includes the features that best fit your user-agent. If using RESTful services, this information will be less important to the web server.

HTTP response

An example of the response that may be returned by the server is this:

```
HTTP/1.1 200 OK                                      (response line)
Content-Type: text/html                              (header
Last-Modified: Sun, 19 Nov 2017 23:11:55 GMT (header)
Content-Length: 138                            (header)
                                               (blank line)
<html>                                         (content)
<head>
  <title>An Example Page</title>
</head>
<body>
  Hello World, this is a very simple HTML document.
</body>
</html>
```

The first line of the response is called the response line, and contains the following information:

- HTTP/1.1: The version of HTTP used; it will always be this when using HTTP 1.1.
- 200: This number is called the status code. The status code is a number telling you what happened at the web service site upon processing your request, and summarizing what it's going to be told to you in the response. There are many status codes and each has its own meaning. 200 means that your request has been handled successfully without any errors, and a response is being shipped to you with the required content. Another popular status code that is known even to non-technical computer users is 404, which means that you requested something that does not exist on the server. 500, for example, means that some errors occurred on the server while processing your request, and so on.
- OK: A text message associated with the response status representing the status in a textual manner; OK is the textual representation of the 200 status code. However, any other message may replace this.

The following lines contain headers. Headers, like in the request, are metadata associated with the response. For example, content-type is used to identify the type of the shipped document with the response; in our example, the response is shipped in HTML format. However, in RESTful web services, responses may be shipped as JSON or XML; this header tells the user-agent what type of response it's holding. MIME types are used to express content types, which are standard web textual representations for different document types.

After headers, a blank line is used to separate headers from the content. Following this blank line, the content we were looking for is shipped.

Although the previous information is very trivial, it's very important to keep in mind a visual of HTTP request and response formats while developing your web services, as the absence of such knowledge will be a mind blocking on your journey in master building web services based systems.

Writing your first REST service

In the following sections, we are going to create our first REST service. Creating a REST service in JAX-RS requires the following two steps:

1. Writing a resource class: A class where we will write our web services methods
2. Configuring Jersey for our project: Telling the application server to load Jersey, and referencing the resource class we will be creating

Writing a resource class

A resource class is the primary building block of RESTful services in JAX-RS. It's a POJO that includes one or more resource methods. Each resource method represents a RESTful service that can be called using one of the main core HTTP methods (GET, POST, PUT, or DELETE).

In order to create a resource class, you will add the @Path annotation to your POJO. The annotation is passed a relative URI that represents the URL of your RESTful service. You will introduce one or more method, annotated with one of the method designator annotations (@GET, @POST, @PUT, or @DELETE).

Let's see an example:

```
@Path("/hello")
public class HelloRest {

    @GET
    public String test() {
        return "Welcome to your first rest service!";
    }
}
```

In the previous code, we have created a RESTful service with the relative URI /hello. The resource can be called using the HTTP GET method, which will be handled using the test() method. By calling /hello with GET, we will have the string Welcome to your first rest service! returned.

That's not everything. We will have also to prepare and configure our project for Jersey, as will be discussed in the next section.

Configuring a project for Jersey

By configuring our project for Jersey, we will be providing two primary pieces of information to the Jersey container:

- The root path of our RESTful services
- The resource classes containing our RESTful services

This can be done by introducing an application configuration class. The application configuration class is a class that extends Jersey's Application class and annotates it with @ApplicationPath. @ApplicationPath tells Jersey which root path we need to use as the root URI for all our RESTful services by passing this information as a parameter to this annotation. Moreover, we will override the getClasses() method, returning a set of classes that are used as resource classes through our application.

Let's see how can we configure our Jersey application:

```java
@ApplicationPath("webresources")
public class ApplicationConfig extends Application {

    @Override
    public Set<Class<?>> getClasses() {
        Set<Class<?>> resources = new java.util.HashSet<>();
        resources.add(HelloRest.class);
        return resources;
    }

}
```

As you can see, we have used the `webresources` URI as the root path of our services. Moreover, we have created a set of `Classes` in the `getClasses()` method, added our `HelloRest` class introduced in the previous section and returned this set back to Jersey.

Now, everything is ready, and our service is ready to be accessed. Our RESTful services will have the following URL:
`http://ip:port/CONTEXT-PATH/ROOT-PATH/SERVICE-PATH`. For the service we introduced in the previous section, it will have the
URL `http://localhost:9354/jaxrs21/webresources/hello`.

Testing your web services

Now, let's test our RESTful service. As we have used the `GET` method for our service, we can test it easily using our ordinary web browser. Just open your favorite web browser, then navigate to the following URL:
`http://localhost:9354/jaxrs21/webresources/hello`

You will get the following output in your browser tab:

```
Welcome to your first rest service!
```

Congratulations! You have just created your first RESTful service.

Postman as a test tool

In the previous section, we tested our RESTful service using a web browser. However, this is not the best tool we normally test our RESTful services with; we will need more advanced tools to test our upcoming RESTful services. One of the most popular tools around is Postman, which introduced an advanced GUI-based interface for testing our RESTful services with very complex scenarios. You can download Postman as a plugin for your Chrome browser, or even install a standalone version. You can get your free copy from `https://www.getpostman.com`.

After installing and launching Postman, you will see the following screen:

As you can see, there is a URL bar similar to those found in web browsers. You can write the URL of our RESTful service there. On the left of this bar, there's a drop-down menu that is used to select the HTTP method we need to test our RESTful service with. For the previous example, we will leave it as GET. The button (**Send**) is used to call the RESTful service, and by calling it, we can see the result in the big box, under the **Body** tab.

Postman is very easy to use, we will explore its other great features in the upcoming sections.

Handling HTTP methods

As mentioned earlier, each HTTP request uses a request method, which in most cases is one of GET, POST, PUT, and DELETE. In RESTful architectures, those HTTP methods are usually used to perform actions based on the following convention:

- GET: Request retrieval of an existing resource
- POST: Request creation of a new resource
- PUT: Request the updating of an existing resource, or create a new one if it does not exist
- DELETE: Request deletion of an existing resource

In JAX-RS, a corresponding annotation for each HTTP method exists @GET, @POST, @PUT, and @DELETE. In the *Handling JSON* section, we will create a complete CRUD example for a RESTful service that performs creation, retrieval, updating, and deletion actions using those methods.

For now, let's try to use each of these methods in a simple example:

```
@Path("/hello")
public class FirstRest {

    @GET
    public String testGet() {
        return "You have issues a get request!";
    }

    @POST
    public String testPost() {
        return "You have issues a post request!";
    }

    @PUT
    public String testPut() {
        return "You have issues a put request!";
    }

    @DELETE
    public String testDelete() {
        return "You have issues a delete request!";
    }

}
```

Using Postman, you can test this service as follows:

1. Launch Postman
2. In the URL input,
   write `http://localhost:9354/jaxrs21/webresources/hello`
3. In the method drop-down at the right of the URL input, choose GET, POST, PUT, and DELETE, and click the **Send** button after each choice
4. Track the output in each case, at the body output below the URL input

To make developing and testing your RESTful services easier, you can save your requests to Postman as follows. For each request method:

1. Click the **Save** button next to send
2. In the request name, write your name of choice, for example, Hello GET
3. In the collection box at the bottom of the screen, click the **Create Collection** link. Collections are used to group your saved requests.

4. Write a name for the collection of your choice, for example, JAX-RS Examples
5. Click the **Save** button

Now, from Postman's main screen, you can navigate to your saved request from the sidebar on the left, click the **JAX-RS Examples** collection and requests will be collapsed, click on your request, and it will be reloaded into the request screen. This way, you can re-run any RESTful service you have developed later, without re-entering request details:

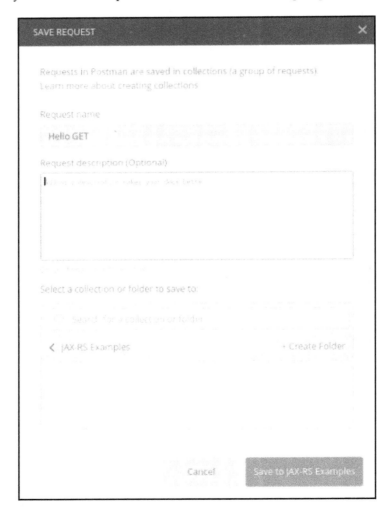

Sub-resources

In JAX-RS, you can also introduce sub-resource functions in the same resources class. Use the @Path annotation to mark one or more functions to be a sub-resource of the original one; the new path will be relative to the original one. Let's see an example:

```
@Path("/hello")
public class FirstRest {

    @Path("/path1")
    @GET
    public String testPath1() {
        return "Hello from path 1!";
    }

    @Path("/path2")
    @GET
    public String testPath2() {
        return "Hello from path 2!";
    }

}
```

As you can see, we have introduced the @Path annotation to the methods testPath1() and testPath2(). The new paths to those methods will be /hello/test1 and /hello/test2 respectively. You can test them using Postman, as we learned earlier.

And, for sure, we can choose the HTTP method of our choice for each of the sub-resource methods, as shown in the following example:

```
@Path("/hello")
public class FirstRest {

    @Path("/path1")
    @GET
    public String testPath1() {
        return "Hello from path 1!";
    }

    @Path("/path2")
    @POST
    public String testPath2() {
        return "Hello from path 2!";
    }

}
```

As you see, we have set the `testPath2()` method to be called using the `POST` method, using the `@POST` annotation.

Receiving parameters

Like any programming function, web services may, and most will be passed various parameters. In JAX-RS, there are different types of parameters that can be passed, including:

- Query parameters
- Path parameters
- Form parameters
- Matrix parameters
- Header parameters

Query parameters

Query parameters are those parameters encoded as a part of the URL by tailing the URL with the question mark symbol `?`, followed by key-value pairs of parameters separated by ampersands, `&`, for example, `http://example.com/add?num1=5num2=6`.

This URL contains two query parameters, called `num1` and `num2`. The values of these parameters are 5 and 6 respectively. The question mark symbol denotes that the rest of the URL is a set of query parameters, separated by ampersands as mentioned earlier. Each parameter has a name, followed by the equals symbol =, followed by the value. If the name or the value has special characters (for example, a question mark, ampersand, equals sign, spaces, or any other URL reserved characters), then a special form of URL encoding will be used. Google *URL encoding* to learn more about how to encode special values in query parameters.

To map query parameters into JAX-RS methods, we shall introduce the parameters as normal Java method parameters first, then annotate them with the `@QueryParam` annotation, passing the name of the expected parameter in the URL query's string, as shown in the following example:

```
@Path("/params")
public class ParamsRest {

    @GET
```

```
public String welcome(@QueryParam("name") String username) {
    return "Welcome " + username + "!";
}

}
```

As you can see, we have introduced a Java parameter called username in the `welcome()` method and annotated it with the `@QueryParameter` annotation, passing `name` as the name of the parameter in the URL query's string. The `welcome()` method takes the username and returns a welcome message to this user. Now, test the service using Postman by writing the following URL:

`http://localhost:9354/jaxrs21/webresources/params?name=Donald`

The following result should be returned from our service:

Welcome Donald!

 Note: In Postman, you don't need to write query parameters directly in the URL input. Click the **Params** button at the right side of the URL input, the parameters section will be collapsed, and you can write your parameters there. The good point is that Postman will perform any special URL encodings required for your parameters if they contain any special characters.

Matrix parameters

Matrix parameters are similar to query parameters; they are encoded as a part of the request URL, but with a different encoding scheme. Matrix parameters are separated by semicolons; , even indicated using a semicolon. An example of them is as follows: `http://example.com/add;num1=5;num2=6`.

This URL contains two matrix parameters, called num1 and num2. The values of these parameters are 5 and 6 respectively. The semicolon symbol denotes that the rest of the URL is a set of query parameters, separated by semicolons also.

To map matrix parameters into JAX-RS methods, we will follow exactly the same steps used with query parameters, but using the `@MatrixParam` annotation, as shown in the following example:

```
@Path("/params")
public class ParamsRest {

    @GET
```

```
public String welcome(@MatrixParam("name") String username) {
    return "Welcome " + username + "!";
}

}
```

Now, test your service with Postman by using the following URL:
`http://localhost:9354/jaxrs21/webresources/params;name=Donald`

The following result should be returned from our service:

Welcome Donald!

You may wonder, what's different between matrix parameters and query parameters, as they both seem to provide the same functionality?

The key difference is that matrix parameters may be applied to a particular path element while query parameters apply to the request as a whole. This comes into play when making a complex REST-style query to multiple levels of resources and sub-resources. For example, consider the following URI call: `http://example.com/movies/categories;name=action/movie;name=foo/?page=1`.

As you can see, each part of the URL has its own matrix parameter; each resource can maintain its own parameters, apart from the sub-resources involved in the same request. You are more than welcome to create your own example and test case to try this feature.

Path parameters

Path parameters are parameters that are included as a part of the request path. For example, the username can be passed as a part of the path as follows:
`http://localhost:9354/jaxrs21/webresources/params/Donald`

As you can see, the username Donald is passed as if it was a part of the URL. This way of passing parameters is very useful when the entity being requested is dynamic, and a generic entity resource handler is used with different types of entities. For example, CRUDing for a list of movies, actors, or producers may be performed using a single resource class, where the type of entity being CRUD itself is passed as a path parameters. It appears to the end user that there exist many different paths for different kinds of resources.

Anyways, let's examine a simple example of this:

```
@Path("/params")
```

```
public class ParamsRest {
    @GET
    @Path("/{name}")
    public String welcome(@PathParam("name") String username) {
        return "Welcome " + username + "!";
    }

}
```

As you can see, we have annotated the `welcome()` method with the `@Path` annotation, passing a path that includes a special parameter name, `name`, enclosed between two curly braces. This way, we tell the JAX-RS implementation that this service includes a path parameter called `name`, which we will map later to a method parameter using the `@PathParam` annotation.

Now, test the service using Postman by typing the following URL: `http://localhost:9354/jaxrs21/webresources/params/Donald`

You should get the following output:

Welcome Donald!

Note that path parameters, like all other parameter types, can be mixed together.

Form parameters

Form parameters are similar to query parameters and are encoded using URL encoding rules, but the difference is that they are sent in the request's payload rather than the URI string. As the name suggests, form parameters are the way HTML forms with the POST method submit data to them.

In JAX-RS, the `@FormParam` annotation is used to map method parameters to form parameters, as shown in the following example:

```
@Path("/params")
public class ParamsRest {

    @POST
    public String testForm(@FormParam("name") String username) {
        return "Welcome " + username + "!";
    }

}
```

To test this REST service using Postman, write the following URI in the URL input: `http://localhost:9354/jaxrs21/webresources/params`

From the body tab below the URL input, select the **Body** tab, then choose **x-www-form-urlencoded**, then write the following key-value pair below this option:

```
name=John
```

Now, click the **Send** button and you will get the following response:

Welcome John!

Header parameters

Parameters can also be passed in headers. Request headers are very commonly used in authentication techniques, such as in OAuth for example. In the following example, we are going to write a REST service that accepts a parameter called `Authorization` in the request header:

```
@Path("/params")
public class ParamsRest {

    @GET
    public String testHeaders(@HeaderParam("Authorization") String
authorization) {
        return "Authorization header value is " + authorization;
    }

}
```

Like other parameter types, we have annotated a method parameter with the `@HeaderParam` annotation, passing `Authorization` as the name of this header. Now, the header is mapped to the method parameter.

Now, let's test this service using Postman. Write the following URI in Postman's URL input field: `http://localhost:9354/jaxrs21/webresources/params`

Then, from the tabs below the Postman URL input field, select the **Headers** tab, then write the following header together with this value:

```
Authorization: Bearer 1234
```

This is a simulation to the authorization header send with all requests in `OAuth2` authentication system. Now, click the **Send** button in Postman and the following result will be returned:

```
Authorization header value is Bearer 1234
```

Providing default values

Parameters can be provided default values, so when the user does not send a value to this parameter with the request, your specified default value will be used. The `@DefaultValue` annotation can be used to provide this default value, passing the value as a string literal, as shown in the following example:

```java
@Path("/params")
public class ParamsRest {

    @GET
    public String welcome(@QueryParam("name")
                          @DefaultValue("John") String username) {
        return "Welcome " + username + "!";
    }
}
```

As you can see, we have annotated the username parameter with the default value `John`. If you tested this service with Postman by using this URL, and without specifying a value for the username parameter: `http://localhost:9354/jaxrs21/webresources/params`

You will get the following output:

```
Welcome John!
```

As you can see, the default value `John` has been used in your request, while the value of this parameter is not passed with the requested content.

Note that even if the parameter type itself is not String, integer, for example, we still should pass the default value to the `@DefaultValue` annotation as a string literal, as it will be converted to the correct type upon request by the JAX-RS provider.

Bean parameters

Bean parameters are a way to encapsulate a set of different types of parameters in one logical class. A bean parameter class is a POJO with attributes annotated with JAX-RS parameter annotations, exactly as shown in earlier points. The bean parameter class can later be used by simply adding it as a parameter to the request's method, annotated with the @BeanParam annotation, as shown in the following example:

```
public class MyBeanParam {

    @PathParam("path")
    private String pathParam;
    @QueryParam("query")
    private String queryParam;
    @HeaderParam("header")
    private String headerParam;
    // getters and setters here

}

@Path("/params")
public class ParamsRest {

    @Path("/{path}")
    @GET
    public String testBeanParams(@BeanParam MyBeanParam myBeanParam){
        return
                "Path Parameter: " + myBeanParam.getPathParam() + "n" +
                "Query Parameter: " + myBeanParam.getQueryParam()+ "n" +
                "Header Parameter: " + myBeanParam.getHeaderParam()+ "n";
    }
}
```

As you can see, the testBeanParams() method is declared with a parameter of type MyBeanParam, annotated with the @BeanParam annotation. The JAX-RS provider will look up for all JAX-RS parameter type annotations inside the bean parameter class, which in our example are:

- A path parameter called path
- A query parameter called query
- A header parameter called header

Now, let's test our REST service using Postman by calling the following URI:

```
GET http://localhost:9354/jaxrs21/webresources/params/x?query=y
Header (header: z)
```

You should get the following output:

```
Path Parameter: x
Query Parameter: y
Header Parameter: z
```

Using context objects

Sometimes, and in some complex RESTful scenarios, you may need to dynamically identify what parameters have been sent to your service at runtime, without knowing in advance what parameters are expected to be sent.

To do so, you can define parameters with the following types within your method, annotated with the @Context annotation:

- **UriInfo:** can be used to obtain all path and query parameters passed to your RESTful service
- **HttpHeaders:** can be used to obtain all HTTP headers passed to your RESTful service

As will be seen in the next example, and with each type of the objects mentioned, parameters are returned as an object of type MultivaluedMap, which is similar to the Java collection's maps, but different in that there can be multiple values for the same parameter name. Therefore, two methods are introduced in this interface:

- getFirst: Returns the first parameter value that occurred for this parameter's name
- get: Returns a list of all parameter values that occurred for this parameter's name

In the following example, we will show an example that dynamically looks for all available path, query, and header parameters, in addition to any cookies associated with the request:

```
@Path("/params")
public class ParamsRest {

    @Path("/{path}")
```

```
@GET
public void testContext(@Context UriInfo uriInfo, @Context
HttpHeaders httpHeaders) {

        MultivaluedMap<String, String> pathParams =
uriInfo.getPathParameters();
        MultivaluedMap<String, String> queryParameters =
uriInfo.getQueryParameters();
        MultivaluedMap<String, String> requestHeaders =
httpHeaders.getRequestHeaders();
        Map<String, Cookie> cookies = httpHeaders.getCookies();

        // process path parameters
        for (String pathParam : pathParams.keySet()) {
            // get the value of the path parameter
            String value = pathParams.getFirst(pathParam);
        }

        // process query parameters
        for (String queryParameter : queryParameters.keySet()) {
            // get the value of the query parameter
            String value = queryParameters.getFirst(queryParameter);

        // get the all the values of the query parameter with this name
            List<String> values = queryParameters.get(queryParameter);
        }

        // process header parameters
        for (String requestHeader : requestHeaders.keySet()) {
            // get the value of the header parameter
            String value = requestHeaders.getFirst(requestHeader);

        // get the all the values of the header parameter with this name
            List<String> values = queryParameters.get(requestHeader);
        }

        // process cookie parameters
        for (String cookieName : cookies.keySet()) {
            Cookie cookie = cookies.get(cookieName);
        }

    }

}
```

It's your own task now to process the passed parameters and test them yourself, have fun!

Handling JSON

JSON is an open, standard, language-independent, text-based data representation format for exchanging data between applications. JSON stands for JavaScript object notation, and as the name suggests, it's the native representation for objects in the JavaScript language. As JavaScript is the primary scripting language for web browsers, JSON is the best choice for sending and delivering data to and from web browsers, as its nativeness gives the best performance for web browsers when parsing and generating data in this format. Moreover, JSON is widely supported by most programming languages, CLI utilities, integration middleware, and so on. Therefore, the JSON format is very widely used in RESTful web APIs.

In the following sections, we are going to learn how to use JSON within our RESTful services.

Enabling Moxy

Moxy is the default and preferred way of supporting JSON with Jersey. Once you add the Moxy dependency to your classpath, Jersey automatically discovers it and adds support to JSON within your Jersey application with no extra effort.

To add the Moxy module, just add the following dependency to your project's pom.xml:

```
<dependency>
    <groupId>org.glassfish.jersey.media</groupId>
    <artifactId>jersey-media-moxy</artifactId>
    <version>2.26</version>
</dependency>
```

Now, your Jersey application supports JSON.

Returning JSON

Let's try to return our first JSON object with JAX-RS. It is so easy that you don't need to handle any special stuff yourself, just return your object from a method declared to return JSON's media type using the @Produces annotation, nothing more!

In the following example, we are going to simulate an in-memory database of movies using a `HashMap`. We are going to create a map of movies, where the key is the movie's id (primary key), and the value is an object representing a movie in some database. We will support two operations in this example:

- Retrieving a movie by `id`
- Listing all movies found in our database

Before we go on with this example, let's discuss how we should design our RESTful services. The dominant convention in the world of rest APIs is the use of what's called resource modeling.

The idea of resource modeling is very simple: any information that can be named is abstracted as a resource. For example, *movies*, the list of all movies, is considered a resource. A single movie is also considered as another resource. Simply, a resource can be a collection (the plural of an object), or singleton (singular object). Each resource has a unique URI; for a collection resource, the convention is to name your resource as, for example, `/movies`. A single resource, which usually falls into the domain of a parent collection, will have the URI `/movies/{movieId}`, where `movieId` is a path parameter inside this collection. It's very common for a sub-resource to have a set of other sub-resources; for example, a movie can have its own actors and can be identified by the URI `/movies/{movieId}/actors`, and so on.

When accessing a resource, there are four basic operations that you usually perform over your resource:

- Retrieving a resource
- Creating a new resource
- Updating a resource
- Deleting a resource

This is very similar to the concept of CRUD, the four basic operations that can be performed over a database. Usually, these operations are mapped to the following HTTP methods:

- **GET:** For retrieving a resource. For example, `GET /movies/11`, should retrieve the movie with the `id` value of `11`.
- **POST:** For creating a new resource. For example, `POST /movies/13`, supplied by a JSON payload representing the movie details, should create a new movie with `id` `13`. Or, a more common case—just posting to `/movies` should create a new resource and return the newly created movie, and/or its generated `id`.

- **PUT:** For updating an existing resource. For example, `PUT /movies/12`, supplied by a JSON payload representing the movie details, should update the movie with `id 12`, with the newly posted object.
- **DELETE:** For deleting an existing resource. For example, `DELETE /movies/13` should delete the movie with `id 13`.

Keep in mind the previous design conventions, as they will be your weapons when designing any REST APIs. In the following example, we are going to implement our RESTful example using those conventions, for retrieving all or a single movie from an in-memory database:

```
public class Movie {

    private long id;
    private String title;

    public Movie() {
    }

    public Movie(long id, String title) {
        this.id = id;
        this.title = title;
    }

    // setters and getters here

}

@Path("movies")
public class MoviesResource {

    private static Map<Long, Movie> moviesDB = new HashMap<>();

    static {
        moviesDB.put(11L, new Movie(11, "Beauty and the Beast"));
        moviesDB.put(12L, new Movie(12, "Suicide Squade"));
    }

    public MoviesResource() {
    }

    @GET
    @Path("/{id}")
    @Produces(MediaType.APPLICATION_JSON)
    public Movie getById(@PathParam("id") long id) {
        return moviesDB.get(id);
```

```
        }
        @GET
        @Produces(MediaType.APPLICATION_JSON)
        public Collection<Movie> listMovies() {
            return moviesDB.values();
        }
    }
```

As you can see, we have defined a static member variable of `HashMap`, simulating an in-memory database of movies. We have used a static initialization block in order to initialize our database with some dummy data.

Moreover, we have defined two functions representing our RESTful APIs:

- `listMovies()`, which is used to list all available movies in our database, mapped to the `/movies` URI. Note that we have not used the `@Path` annotation with this function, and therefore it will be mapped to the default one for the resource class, which is `/movies`.
- `GetById()`, which is used to retrieve a movie by its `id`. This function is mapped to the URI `/movies/{id}`, where the movie `id` will be passed as a path parameter to this URI.

For both methods, we have introduced the `@Produces` annotation, passing `MediaType.APPLICATION_JSON`, which maps to the MIME type `application/json`. This annotation will do all the magic for returning our data in the JSON format. Jersey will use Moxy's JSON engine to format our output from those methods using the JSON format.

You can also see that we have followed the resource modeling design conventions mentioned earlier, and it's time to see them in action now. Let's try to retrieve all of our movies by calling the following URI using Postman:
`http://localhost:9354/jaxrs21/webresources/movies`

You should get the following output:

```
[
    {
        "id": 11,
        "title": "Beauty and the Beast"
    },
    {
        "id": 12,
        "title": "Suicide Squad"
    }
]
```

Now, let's try to retrieve the movie information with `id 11` by calling the following URL using Postman: `http://localhost:9354/jaxrs21/webresources/movies/11`

You will get the following output:

```
{
    "id": 11,
    "title": "Beauty and the Beast"
}
```

Once again, but using `id 12`:
`http://localhost:9354/jaxrs21/webresources/movies/12`

You will have the following output:

```
{
    "id": 12,
    "title": "Suicide Squade"
}
```

Consuming JSON

In the following example, we are going to complement the previous one by supporting, creating, and updating movies within the movies resources class. According to the convention we agreed on, we will use the `@POST` method for creating a new movie and the `@PUT` method for updating an existing one.

Receiving a JSON payload and converting it to an object using JAX-RS is as easy as annotating your method with `@Consumes(MediaType.APPLICATION_JSON)` and introducing a parameter of your required object type. The annotation tells the JAX-RS provider to accept a JSON payload and convert it to the object type that appears as your method's parameter.

Let's add the following code to the `MoviesResouce` class:

```
@Path("movies")
public class MoviesResource {

    ....

    @PUT
    @Path("/{id}")
    @Consumes(MediaType.APPLICATION_JSON)
    public void modifyById(@PathParam("id") long id, Movie movie) {
```

```
        if (!moviesDB.containsKey(id)) {
            throw new RuntimeException("No movie with such id found!");
        }
        moviesDB.put(id, movie);
    }

    @POST
    @Consumes(MediaType.APPLICATION_JSON)
    public void addMovie(Movie movie) {
        if (moviesDB.containsKey(movie.getId())) {
            throw new RuntimeException("A movie with such id already
exists!");
        }
        moviesDB.put(movie.getId(), movie);
    }
}
```

As you can see, we have introduced two new methods:

- addMovie(): Used to add a new movie to the in-memory database. The method has a parameter of type Movie, which is used to accept a payload of type JSON containing movie information.
- modifyById: Used to update an existing movie in the in-memory database. The method has two parameters:
  - id: A path parameter that contains the id of the movie to update
  - A movie object: The payload of the movie information to be updated

Now, let's try to test our two new methods. Using Postman, call the following URI with the shown HTTP method and BODY content:

```
PUT http://localhost:9354/jaxrs21/webresources/movies/12

BODY
{
    "id": 12,
    "title": "Suicide Squade [Modified]"
}
```

We have updated the movie with id 12 with a new title. Now, call the following URI with the shown information:

```
POST http://localhost:9354/jaxrs21/webresources/movies/13

BODY
```

```
{
    "id": 13,
    "title": "New Movie"
}
```

We have created a new movie with `id` 13 and the title `New Movie`. Now, call the following URI to see a list of all available movies:

```
GET http://localhost:9354/jaxrs21/webresources/movies
```

You will get the following result:

```
[
  {
    "id": 11,
    "title": "Beauty and the Beast"
  },
  {
    "id": 12,
    "title": "Suicide Squade [Modified]"
  },
  {
    "id": 13,
    "title": "New movie"
  }
]
```

Custom responses

As discussed earlier, any response from a RESTful service may include:

- Status code
- Response entity
- Content type

By default, any RESTful service that runs and returns normally without any problems will contain the status code `200` (OK). The response entity will be these value you return from the RESTful method. The content type will be these one specified by the `@Produces` annotation, as mentioned earlier.

Sometimes, you may need to customize the details of the response yourself at runtime, in one of the following scenarios:

- The response entity data type/MIME content type is not known until runtime
- A custom status code should be returned to the client according to some business logic inside the RESTful service code

In JAX-RS, you can customize the response at runtime by following two steps:

1. Declaring the return type of the method to be of type `Response`
2. Building a custom response object from inside your RESTful service code and returning it to the client

Building a `response` object is easy and can be done in one statement, as follows:

```
Response.status(STATUS_CODE).entity(RESPONSE_CONTENT).build();
```

`STATUS_CODE` and `RESPONSE_CONTENT` are passed as parameters to the methods shown in the previous code snippet. If the method returns with an error, a custom status type indicating what types of errors occurred should be passed. If your method runs without any errors, you can return the status code `200` (OK), indicating that you are returning normally without any problems. This can be done in a shorthand way as follows:

```
Response.ok(RESPONSE_CONTENT).build();
```

Moreover, you can pass a custom MIME type to define the type of the content of your response, as follows:

```
Response.ok(RESPONSE_CONTENT, RESPONSE_CONTENT_TYPE).build();
```

Let's apply this to a real-world example. In the following example, we are going to create an images resource class that delivers a requested image to from the server to the client by locating some given image name at a known directory on the server, then returning the image back to the client.

Our service will work as follows. The client will request the image by calling the following URI:

```
GET http://localhost:9354/jaxrs21/webresources/images/[IMAGE_FILE_NAME]
```

The server should respond as follows:

- If the image is not found on the server, it should return status 404, indicating that the content is not found
- If the image is found on the server, the image's byte contents should be returned to the client, with the appropriate content type: `image/jpg`, `image/png`, or `image/gif`
- If the image is found but an I/O error occurred during retrieval, a response with status `500` (internal server error) should be returned

The following example implements this scenario:

```
@Path("/images")
public class ImagesResource {

    @GET
    @Path("/{imageName}")
    public Response renderImage(@PathParam("imageName") String imageName) {

        // create a file object referencing the expected image path
        // replae /path/to/images with a real path on your file system
File imageFile = new File("/path/to/images/" + imageName);

        // if file does not exist, return 404 error!
        if (!imageFile.exists()) {
            return Response.status(Status.NOT_FOUND)
                    .entity("Image not fouund")
                    .build();
        }

        // extract image extension
        int extIndex = imageFile.getName().lastIndexOf('.');
        String ext = imageFile.getName().substring(extIndex +
1).toLowerCase();

        try {
            // convert extension to a mime type using a utility method
            String mime = getMimeType(ext);

            // return the image's stream, together with its mime type
            return Response.ok(new FileInputStream(imageFile),
mime).build();
        } catch (IllegalArgumentException ex) {
            // extension is not known to be image, return 404 error!
            return Response.status(Status.NOT_FOUND)
                    .entity("Unknown image type!").build();
```

```
        } catch (IOException ex) {
            // I/O error occurred, return 500 error!
            return Response.status(Status.INTERNAL_SERVER_ERROR)
                .entity("I/O error occured!").build();
        }
    }

    private String getMimeType(String ext) {
        if ("jpg".equals(ext)) {
            return "image/jpg";
        } else if ("png".equals(ext)) {
            return "image/png";
        } else if ("gif".equals(ext)) {
            return "image/gif";
        } else {
            throw new IllegalArgumentException("Unkown exception!");
        }
    }
}
```

Now, let's test our service. Copy your favorite image to your images path on your local filesystem, with, for example, the name `test.jpg`, then using Postman, call the following URI: `http://localhost:9354/jaxrs21/webresources/images/test.jpg`

You should see your favorite image displayed in Postman; fortunately, it supports displaying images returned from the web server. Let's check the content type returned by selecting the `Headers` tab from the response block, and you should see:

```
Content-Type: image/jpg
```

Now, let's try to access an image that does not exist by calling the following URI: `http://localhost:9354/jaxrs21/webresources/images/nothing.jpg`

You should see the status `404` not found in Postman.

Uploading files

Uploading files are one of the most important aspects of RESTful services. Embedding file contents as binary data within an HTTP request that is text-based is supported using multi-part requests. As the name suggests, a multi-part request is a request containing many parts; some of the parts are text, and others may include binary data. The internal details of multi-part requests are out of the scope of this book. However, you can Google *HTTP Multi-Part* to learn more about the internals of HTTP multi-part requests.

To use multi-part requests within your Jersey application, you should first include a multi-part support library within your application by adding the following dependency in your project's pom.xml file:

```
<dependency>
    <groupId>org.glassfish.jersey.media</groupId>
    <artifactId>jersey-media-multipart</artifactId>
    <version>2.26</version>
</dependency>
```

Then, you should register MultiPartFeature to your Jersey's application context, as shown in the following excerpt:

```
@ApplicationPath("webresources")
public class ApplicationConfig extends Application {

    @Override
    public Set<Class<?>> getClasses() {
        Set<Class<?>> resources = new java.util.HashSet<>();
        ....
        resources.add(MultiPartFeature.class);
        return resources;
    }

}
```

Now, recalling the image resource example, we will modify the image resource class to add support for uploading images via a POST requests. Let's see what the code should look like:

```
@Path("/images")
public class ImagesResource {

    ....
    @POST
    @Consumes(MediaType.MULTIPART_FORM_DATA)
    public Response uploadImage(
            @FormDataParam("imageFile") InputStream imageFileStream,
            @FormDataParam("imageFile") FormDataContentDisposition
fileDisposition) {
        File imageFile = new File("/path/to/images/" +
fileDisposition.getFileName());

        // if the file with the same name already exists, returns an
error
        if (imageFile.exists()) {
            return Response.status(Status.BAD_REQUEST)
                    .entity("Image with the same name already exists!")
```

```
                    .build();
        }

        try {
            // create a file output stream to write uploaded file
contents
            // to the server's file system
            FileOutputStream fos = new FileOutputStream(imageFile);

            // read the submitted file as chunks, and write to the
server's file
            byte[] buff = new byte[5 * 1024];
            int len;
            while ((len = imageFileStream.read(buff)) != -1) {
                fos.write(buff, 0, len);
            }
            fos.close();

            // return a success message to the client
            return Response.ok("Image uploaded successfully!").build();
        } catch (IOException ex) {
            return Response.status(Status.INTERNAL_SERVER_ERROR)
                    .entity("I/O error occured!").build();
        }
    }
}
```

As you can see, we have introduced a method called `uploadImage()`. The method is annotated with `@Consumes(MediaType.MULTIPART_FORM_DATA)`, which tells the JAX-RS provider that our RESTful service is expecting a request of multi-part type (that is, including a binary file content). The method introduces two parameters:

- `imageFileStream`: An input stream that holds uploaded file data; the annotation `@FormDataParam("imageFile")` tells the JAX-RS provider that the name of this parameter in the requested content is called `imageFile`.
- `fileDisposition`: An object of type `FormDataFileDisposition` containing key submitted file information, such as the filename. This parameter is annotated the same as the previous one.

The implementation of the method reads the submitted file content then writes it to the server's filesystem, as explained in the code comments. Don't forget to change the root path to a real path in your local filesystem.

Now, let's try to upload test this method. In Postman, write the following URI in the URL input: `http://localhost:9354/jaxrs21/webresources/images`

In the method's drop-down, choose `POST`, then select the **Body** tab, make sure the form-data radio is selected, then from the parameters list below, include a parameter with the key `imageFile`, and next to parameter name, change **Text** to **File**. Then, in the value input, click **Choose Files**; this will open the file choice popup and you can select an image from your filesystem. Now, click **Send**, then check the existence of your uploaded image in your selected path.

Handling exceptions

Exceptions are as important to handle in RESTful services as in any normal programming code. Errors in RESTful services should be mapped to the appropriate response code, as shown in the image retrieval example. JAX-RS provides a generic way of mapping Java exceptions to custom responses to the way you design. There are two approaches to mapping Java exceptions to HTTP responses:

- Declaring custom web application exceptions
- Mapping existing exceptions to error responses

In the following sections, we are going to examine each of the two approaches.

Declaring custom web application exceptions

Web application exceptions are a custom type of exception, customized for JAX-RS to include a fully-detailed response with this exception. To declare your own, just create a class extending the `WebApplicationException` class and pass to the `super`'s constructor an instance of the response class with your desired content that describes the error details, as discussed in the *Custom responses* section. Let's see an example of this:

```
public class MyException extends WebApplicationException {

    public MyException() {
        super(Response.status(Response.Status.BAD_REQUEST)
.build());
    }

    public MyException(String message) {
        super(Response.status(Response.Status.BAD_REQUEST)
                .entity(message)
```

```
                    .type(MediaType.TEXT_PLAIN)
                    .build());
        }
    }
```

As you can see, we have declared two constructors, one with zero-args that pass to the superclass a response with status code 400 (Bad Request), and another one with a string argument that does as the first constructor but associates a custom message with our exception.

Now, let's put the web application exception into action. Recalling the CRUD example shown in the *Consuming JSON* example, we will modify the code of the modifyById method to return an instance of MyException when the client tries to issue an update command to a movie with a key that does not exist:

```
@Path("movies")
public class MoviesResource {

    . . .

    @PUT
    @Consumes(MediaType.APPLICATION_JSON)
    public void modifyById(Movie movie) {
        if (!moviesDB.containsKey(movie.getId())) {
            throw new MyException("No movie with such id found!");
        }
        moviesDB.put(id, movie);
    }

    . . .

}
```

Now, it's your own task to test this method with an invalid parameter using Postman, with a request similar to our examples used in this section, and examine the error response yourself.

Mapping existing exceptions

This approach provides an easier way to map your Java exceptions to custom RESTful responses. You can declare a predefined mapping for all your desired Java exceptions to custom rest responses. Whenever an exception for these is thrown from any RESTful service, the JAX-RS provider will automatically generate your predefined request.

For each Java exception that you expect to be thrown from your RESTful services, you will follow two steps:

1. Define an exception mapper provider class
2. Register the provider within the JAX-RS application context

In the following example, we are going to map `java.lang.ArithmeticException` to a custom HTTP response. Let's follow the first step, which is defining an exception mapper provider class, as follows:

```
@Provider
public class ArithmeticExceptionMapper implements
ExceptionMapper<ArithmeticException> {

    @Override
    public Response toResponse(ArithmeticException ex) {
        return Response.status(Status.BAD_REQUEST).
                entity(ex.getMessage()).
                type(MediaType.TEXT_PLAIN).
                build();
    }
}
```

As you see, the exception mapper provider class implements the `ExceptionMapper` interface, passing the desired exception as a generic parameter to it, which in our case is the `ArithmeticException` class. Then, we have overridden the abstract `toReponse()` method of the `ExceptionMapper` interface; we use this method to define how this exception will be converted to a custom response, which in our case returned a response with error `400` (Bad Request) associated with a custom message with the same that is shown in the exception object itself.

Now, let's follow the second step, which is to register the provider class in the JAX-RS application context. We will modify the `ApplicationConfig` class as follows:

```
@ApplicationPath("webresources")
public class ApplicationConfig extends Application {

    @Override
    public Set<Class<?>> getClasses() {
        Set<Class<?>> resources = new java.util.HashSet<>();
        ....
        resources.add(CalculatorResource.class);
        resources.add(ArithmeticExceptionMapper.class);
```

```
        return resources;
    }

}
```

As you see, we have added the `ArithmeticExceptionMapper` class to the set of resources. Now, let's try this custom mapping in action. We will press on with this example by creating a simple division calculator service that takes two integer parameters, x and y, then returns the result of dividing x by y. If we pass zero as the value of y, then `ArithmeticException` will occur. According to our mapping, an error response with status 400 (Bad Request), with the message / by zero, will be returned. The code of the RESTful service will be as follows:

```
@Path("/calculator")
public class CalculatorResource {

    @Path("/divide")
    @GET
    public int divide(@QueryParam("x") int x,
            @QueryParam("y") int y) {
        return x / y;
    }
}
```

Now, let's test this service with Postman by calling the following URI:
`http://localhost:9354/jaxrs21/webresources/calculator/divide?x=5&y=0`

The output will be as follows:

```
Status: 400 Bad Request
/ by zero.
```

Server-sent events

The classic model of HTTP communication is the single-request-response model: the client issues a request to the server, the server sends a response, the connection gets closed, that's all! Each HTTP connection serves exactly one response.

In some scenarios, the opposite of this model is required—the server sends some data to the client, without a special request from the client. This is very common in notification systems, such as social media notification pop-ups, or in applications such as chatting. When the client has a new notification or a chatting message, the server should redirect it to the client.

It is technically impossible for the server to initiate a connection to the client; therefore, some techniques were invented to support this model, which we are going to summarize as follows:

- **Polling:** The client repeatedly requests new content from the server. For example, in a chatting application, the client will issue a request each second to check for new messages coming from the server. If there are new messages, the server will send them as a response. Otherwise, the server will send nothing to the client. In both cases, the connection gets terminated.

- **Long-polling:** The client repeatedly requests new content from the server, but if there is no new content from the server, the connection gets held and the server never responds until new content is available to be sent back to the client. In other words, the connection never gets terminated after the initial request until new content is ready to be sent. After connection termination, the client will issue a new request.

- **Web sockets:** A technique for opening a full-duplex two-way communication channel, such as the usual sockets used in low-level network programming applications, but over an HTTP request. There will be a separate chapter on this topic in this book.

- **Server-sent events:** A technique similar to long polling, but different in that when a client issues a request, the connection stays alive and for every new ready message, the message will be sent to the client while keeping the original connection open. In other words, a single connection is used to track any new updates coming from the server. This introduces a very simple and straightforward model for keeping the client updated with any new updates from the server it's interested in.

Before JAX-RS 2.1, there was no standard API for handling SSE in Java EE. Now in JAX-RS 2.1, there is a built-in support for this technique, which would be very useful in building trendy applications seamlessly with the standard Java EE APIs.

To create an SSE service, you will create a normal JAX-RS resource class, introduce your handler method, and annotate it with `@Produces(MediaType.SERVER_SENT_EVENTS)`, telling the JAX-RS provider that you are going to respond to the client from this service using the SSE technique.

You will introduce two parameters in your method, both annotated with the `@Context` annotation, with the following types:

- **SseEventSink:** The object used to return things from your service to your client. As you are returning more than one response, this object is used to send a response to your client each time you have some new data ready to be sent, rather than a regular Java method return. Your method will be void, and this object will be used for returning instead.
- **Sse:** The object used to prepare a response object to be sent to the client via the `SseEventSink` object discussed in the previous point.

In the following example, we are going to create an SSE service that returns 10 hello world messages; each subsequent message will be delayed for one second, simulating a waiting time for new content to be ready on the server:

```
@Path("/events")
public class SseResource {

    @GET
    @Produces(MediaType.SERVER_SENT_EVENTS)
    public void testSSE(@Context SseEventSink eventSink, @Context Sse
sse) {
        new Thread(() -> {
            for (int i = 0; i < 10; i++) {

                // prepare a new message to be sent to the client
                final OutboundSseEvent event = sse.newEventBuilder()
                        .name("message")
                        .data(String.class, "Hello world " + i + "!")
                        .build();

                // send the new message to the client
                eventSink.send(event);

                // wait for one second before the next message
                try {
                    Thread.sleep(1000);
                } catch (InterruptedException e) {}
            }
        }).start();
    }
}
```

As you can see, we have created an SSE service, bound to the URI /events, with the testSSE() method mapped to the @GET method, and produced a server-sent event. The method introduces the parameters discussed earlier, which are used inside our method's implementation.

The method creates a thread that initiates a loop with 10 iterations, each iteration delayed for one second, using the Thread.sleep() method. In each iteration, we have used the SSE object to build a new response message. The builder pattern is very similar to the one we used with regular Response objects: we use a builder methods chain, tailed by build(), to build our message. We gave the message the name message; this name is used as a discriminator by the client side to differentiate between each message type if there are different ones. We have also included the data, which is of type String and contains a *Hello World* message concatenated with a number from the loop counter. If an SSE client connects to this event's endpoint, it will receive a new message every second.

Now, as Postman does not support testing SSE events at the time of writing, let's create an interesting example of consuming the SSE service using a real web page, with JavaScript. Create a web page with the name stream-client.html in your project with the following code:

```html
<!DOCTYPE html>
<html>
    <head>
        <title>Stream Client</title>
        <meta http-equiv="Content-Type" content="text/html;
charset=UTF-8">
    </head>
    <body>
        <h1>Server-Sent Events Test</h1>
        <div id="messages">
            <!--Server sent messages will be displayed here!-->
        </div>

        <script
src="https://code.jquery.com/jquery-3.2.1.min.js"></script>
        <script>
            if (window.EventSource) {
                // create a new event source object to listen to new
                // events sent from our SSE service
                var source = new
EventSource('/jaxrs21/webresources/events');

                // add an event listener to track messages with name
    "message"
                source.addEventListener('message', function (e) {
```

```
                        // append the new message as a paragraph inside
                         // the messages div
                        $('#messages').append('<p>' + e.data + '</p?');
                    }, false);

                } else {
                    window.alert("Event source is not supported by your
browser!");
                }

            </script>
        </body>
    </html>
```

In the previous example, we created an event source object with JavaScript that references the URI of our SSE service, then listens for any messages with the name `message` coming from our service. For each new message, we have used jQuery to append a paragraph object to a message container `div` defined with `id` `#messages`. Running the previous example in your web browser, you will get the following output, but with a time gap of one second between each line:

Server-Sent Events Test

Hello world 0!
Hello world 1!
Hello world 2!
Hello world 3!
Hello world 4!
Hello world 5!
Hello world 6!
Hello world 7!
Hello world 8!
Hello world 9!

Summary

In this chapter, we learned how to create and call RESTful web services. This is a very important step in your journey toward building an enterprise application. It's very important to recall that JSON is a very important player in this field, and therefore we should have a separate chapter about it. In the next chapter, we are going to learn different techniques for playing with JSON data, using the newly introduced API, JSON-B 1.0.

Manipulating JSON with JSON-B 1.0

6

Object serialization and deserialization are one of the primary operations in any enterprise application. Object states are required to be serialized in order to be transformed from one system to another over a network connection, and the other system needs to deserialize the object in order to construct it back and start processing its state. This is a primary concept in remote procedure calls performed in distributed systems.

Although JSON is one of the top essentials in distributed systems communication, there was no standard Java APIs for parsing and generating JSON until Java EE 8. Of course, third-party libraries such as Jackson and GSON have existed for many years, but Java EE 8 finally introduced the standard **JSON-B (JSON Binding)** API, which is very similar in the name and concepts of the **JAXB (Java API for XML Binding)** API.

In this chapter, we are going to explore the JSON-B API, and the different features and configurations provided to our application to parse and generate JSON content. In the following sections, we are going to cover the following:

- Why JSON?
- Mapping our Java objects to JSON
- Mapping Java collections to JSON
- Formatting JSON output
- Customizing property names, ordering, and naming strategy
- Handling special values such as nulls, dates, and times
- Using binary data within JSON documents

Why JSON?

Although Java has provided a native serialization mechanism since the early versions, implementing the marker interface Serializable, which is the default choice for RMIs performed through remote EJB calls, results in the following drawbacks:

- Class versioning problems: Objects may fail to be deserialized if a different version of the class is loaded in the two communicating systems, and/or a different classloader is used in both
- Platform-specific: Java object serialization, as the name suggests, is a Java proprieties technique; other systems written in other languages are not able to easily consume Java objects without the need to use third-party libraries

A standard serialization technique is a must for communication between different systems written in different languages in a heterogeneous environment. XML and JSON are two popular text-based standard formats that have been used for this purpose for many years. XML was the primary technology that modern web techniques built around, such as AJAX and SOAP services, however, JSON has gained more popularity and preferences from system architects in recent years for the following reasons:

- JSON has a smaller fingerprint than XML. As XML is too verbose, JSON is more suitable for network communication; it saves bandwidth of limited data usage, and result in a better performance
- JSON is much quicker than XML to be parsed in web browsers—JSON stands for JavaScript object notation, and, as the name suggests, it's the native representation for objects in JavaScript, and therefore it's quicker than any other format to be parsed in web-based applications

 JSON usage has also been expanded to other interesting areas in the information technology field, for example, data modeling in NoSQL databases (such as Mongo) and search engines (such as Elastic).

Mapping objects

The first thing to learn in JSON-B API, is basically mapping Java objects from/to JSON strings. The entry point to use mapping and other JSON-B features are the `Jsonb` object. The `Jsonb` object is instantiated through a `JsonbBuilder` class, as will be shown in the following example.

After creating the `jsonb` object, the methods `toJson()` and `fromJson()` serialize an object to a JSON string and deserialize an object from a JSON string, respectively. In the following example, we will show how to serialize a movie object into a JSON string:

```
public class Movie {

    private long id;
    private String title;

    // setters and getters here

}

// instantiating a jsonb object
Jsonb jsonb = JsonbBuilder.create();
jsonb.toJson(jsonb);

//creating a movie object
Movie movie = new Movie();
movie.setId(15);
movie.setTitle("Beauty and The Beast");

// mapping the movie object into a json string
String json = jsonb.toJson(movie);
System.out.println(json);
```

By running the previous example, you will get the following output:

```
{"id":15,"title":"Beauty and The Beast"}
```

This is the JSON representation of the `movie` object that we have just created. Note that JSON attributes hold the same names as object attributes do.

Now, let's do the reverse operation—deserializing the JSON string back into a Java object:

```
String json = "{"id":15,"title":"Beauty and The Beast"}";
Jsonb jsonb = JsonbBuilder.create();

Movie movie = jsonb.fromJson(json, Movie.class);
System.out.println("Movie ID: " + movie.getId());
System.out.println("Movie Title: " + movie.getTitle());
```

As you can see, we have called from the JSON method, passing two parameters:

- The JSON string, which contains the object state
- The object type of the JSON data passed

By running the previous example, we will get the following output:

```
Movie ID: 15
Movie Title: Beauty and The Beast
```

We have printed the object state after deserializing it from the JSON string, and we see here that state has been extracted from JSON successfully.

Mapping collections

Collections can also be mapped from/to JSON arrays. In the following example, we will create a collection of multiple JSON objects, and then serialize it into a JSON array:

```
Movie movie1 = new Movie();
movie1.setId(15);
movie1.setTitle("Beauty and The Beast");

Movie movie2 = new Movie();
movie2.setId(16);
movie2.setTitle("The Boss Baby");

Movie movie3 = new Movie();
movie3.setId(17);
movie3.setTitle("Suicide Squad");

// creating a list of the movie objects
List<Movie> movies = new ArrayList<>();
movies.add(movie1);
movies.add(movie2);
movies.add(movie3);

Jsonb jsonb = JsonbBuilder.create();
jsonb.toJson(jsonb);

// convert to json
String json = jsonb.toJson(movies);
System.out.println(json);
```

By running the previous example, we will have the following output:

```
[{"id":15,"title":"Beauty and The Beast"},{"id":16,"title":"The Boss
Baby"},{"id":17,"title":"Suicide Squad"}]
```

In order to deserialize a JSON array back into a collection, we will also use the toJson method. The tricky part is choosing the type passed to the method. In this example, we will create an instance of an anonymous inner class of type ArrayList<Movie>, then we will call getGenericSuperClass() of the type of this new inner class. This way, we can define to the toJson string that we need to retrieve the results in ArrayList<String> specifically, as shown in the following example:

```
String json = "[{"id":15,"title":"Beauty and The
Beast"},{"id":16,"title":"The Boss Baby"},{"id":17,"title":"Suicide
Squad"}]";
Jsonb jsonb = JsonbBuilder.create();

ArrayList<Movie> list = jsonb.fromJson(json, new
ArrayList<Movie>(){}.getClass().getGenericSuperclass());

for (Movie movie : list) {
    System.out.println("Movie ID: " + movie.getId());
    System.out.println("Movie Name: " + movie.getTitle());
    System.out.println();
}
```

As we have looped over the list after deserialization, we have then printed the state of each movie object. By running the previous example, the output will be as follows:

```
Movie ID: 15
Movie Name: Beauty and The Beast

Movie ID: 16
Movie Name: The Boss Baby

Movie ID: 17
Movie Name: Suicide Squad
```

Formatting output

Some configuration parameters can be used to change the behavior of the JSON serialization/deserialization process. This is done by passing a JSON `config` object to the `create` method of the `JsonBuilder` class. The configuration object is used to hold some configuration metadata, which the `jsonb` object will be used during serialization/deserialization.

In the following example, we will create a JSON `config` object to be used within the `jsonb` object:

```
// Instantiate a custom JSON-B configuration object
JsonbConfig config = new JsonbConfig();


// Instantiate a JSON-B object with our custom configuration
Jsonb jsonb = JsonbBuilder.create(config);
```

We have not performed any changes to the default configuration values of the `jsonb` configuration object. Now, let's enable one of the pretty features of `jsonb`, which is the formatting option.

The formatting option is used to format the output JSON, so that it's displayed with hierarchy and indentation to make it more readable by humans. Let's see an example:

```
JsonbConfig config = new JsonbConfig().withFormatting(true);
Jsonb jsonb = JsonbBuilder.create(config);

Movie movie = new Movie();
movie.setId(15);
movie.setTitle("Beauty and The Beast");

String json = jsonb.toJson(movie);
System.out.println(json);
```

As you can see, we have enabled the formatting object by calling `withFormatting`, passing a true value as a parameter to it. By running the previous example, we will have the following output:

```
{
    "id": 15,
    "title": "Beauty and The Beast"
}
```

As you can see, now JSON is more human-readable. The curly braces are printed on separate lines, and each attribute is printed on a separate line, with an indentation.

Customizing property names

As shown earlier, the default behavior of JSON serialization is to use the attribute names as they're found in the class, as the attribute names of the resultant JSON object. It's very common that you may need to change the resulting property name, according to the project's specification. Therefore, the `@JsonbProperty` annotation is available to be used on class fields, in order to provide custom names for the annotated attributes in the resulting JSON string.

Let's try customizing the property name of the movie's title in the following example:

```java
public class Movie {

    private long id;
    @JsonbProperty("movie-title")
    private String title;

    // getters and setters here

}

JsonbConfig config = new JsonbConfig().withFormatting(true);
Jsonb jsonb = JsonbBuilder.create(config);

Movie movie = new Movie();
movie.setId(15);
movie.setTitle("Beauty and The Beast");

String json = jsonb.toJson(movie);
System.out.println(json);
```

By running the previous example, the output JSON will be as follows:

```
{
"id": 15,
"movie-title": "Beauty and The Beast"
}
```

As you can see, the name of the JSON attribute has become "move-title" rather than `title`, as has been used in the default implementation. `@JsonbProperty` also takes effect when deserializing JSON strings back into Java objects.

Customizing naming strategies

Rather than configuring the property name in the JSON string for each attribute specifically, you can define a general naming strategy globally to be applied on all the JSON attributes. This is done by using the property naming strategy option in the `jsonb` configuration object, while creating the `jsonb` object. Let's see an example of this:

```
public class Movie {

    private long id;
    private String title;
    private int productionYear;

    // getters and setters here

}

JsonbConfig config =
        new JsonbConfig()
.withPropertyNamingStrategy
                    (PropertyNamingStrategy.UPPER_CAMEL_CASE)
            .withFormatting(true);
Jsonb jsonb = JsonbBuilder.create(config);

Movie movie = new Movie();
movie.setId(15);
movie.setTitle("Beauty and The Beast");
movie.setProductionYear(2017);

String json = jsonb.toJson(movie);
System.out.println(json);
```

As you can see in the previous example, we have used the `withPropertyNameingStrategy()` method while creating the `jsonb` configuration object. This method used the default naming strategy by using the `jsonb` process while serializing/deserializing objects, which is using the same names found in the Java fields. We have passed `PropertyNamingStrategy.UPPER_CAMEL_CASE`, which means that we need to use all attribute names with the upper camel case notation, which means using the first word of each word found in the Java Field name capital, including the first letter.

By running the previous example, the output JSON will be as follows:

```
{
    "Id": 15,
    "ProductionYear": 2017,
    "Title": "Beauty and The Beast"
}
```

As you can notice, all JSON attribute names now start with capital letters.

The following table lists all the available naming strategies available in the JSON-B specification, along with their explanation:

Naming Strategy	Explanation
IDENTITY	The property name is used as it appears in the Java class. For example, a `birthDate` Java field will appear as `birthDate` in the resulting JSON.
LOWER_CASE_WITH_DASHES	The property name is generated in lowercase letters, with dashes as a separator between words. For example, a `birthDate` Java field will appear as `birth-date` in the resulting JSON.
LOWER_CASE_WITH_UNDERSCORES	The property name is generated in lowercase letters, with an underscore as a separator between words. For example, a `birthDate` Java field will appear as `birth_date` in the resulting JSON.
UPPER_CAMEL_CASE	The property name is generated in one part, with the first word in uppercase. For example, a `birthDate` Java field will appear as `BirthDate` in the resulting JSON.
UPPER_CAMEL_CASE_WITH_SPACES	The property name is generated in first-letter capital form for each word, with a space as a separator between words. For example, a `birthDate` Java field will appear as `birthDate` in the resulting JSON.
CASE_INSENSITIVE	The property name is used as it in the Java class. For example, a `birthDate` Java field will appear as `birthDate` in the resulting JSON. But when deserializing a Java object from a JSON string, the `jsonb` processor will be case-sensitive, ignoring any differences in capitalization.

Customizing property ordering

The order of properties appearing in the resulting JSON can also be customized using the `@JsonbPropertyOrder` annotation on the Java classes. For example, we can use the lexical order, as shown in the following example:

```
@JsonbPropertyOrder(PropertyOrderStrategy.LEXICOGRAPHICAL)
public class Movie {
    . . . .
}
```

Upon serializing the previous object, the resulting JSON attributes will be displayed sorted in alphabetical order; you can try this yourself.

There are three available values for the property order configuration property, as shown in the following table with an explanation for each:

Order Strategy	Explanation
ANY	The resulting JSON attributes are not guaranteed to be in any specific order.
LEXICOGRAPHICAL	The resulting JSON attributes are shown in alphabetical order.
REVERSE	The resulting JSON attributes are shown in reverse alphabetical order.

Ignoring properties

In some cases, you may need to ignore some Java object properties from being displayed in the resulting JSON string; they may be non-primary properties holding temporary values, or some internal attributes that will not be interesting to the JSON consumer party. Hence, the `@JsonbTransient` annotation is used to hide some Java attributes from being shown in the resulting JSON, as shown in the following examples:

```
public class Movie {

    private long id;
    private String title;
    @JsonbTransient
    private int productionYear;

    // setters and getters here
}

JsonbConfig config = new JsonbConfig().withFormatting(true);
Jsonb jsonb = JsonbBuilder.create(config);
```

```
Movie movie = new Movie();
movie.setId(15);
movie.setTitle("Beauty and The Beast");
movie.setProductionYear(2017);

String json = jsonb.toJson(movie);
System.out.println(json);
```

By running the previous example, the output will be as follows:

```
{
    "id": 15,
    "title": "Beauty and The Beast"
}
```

As you can see, we have annotated the `productionYear` property of the `Movie` class with a `@JsonbTransient` attribute. Therefore, the value of `productionYear` has not been shown in the resulting JSON.

Handling nulls

Null values can be handled in one of two ways with JSON-B:

- Properties with null values are not shown in the resulting JSON string
- Properties with null values are shown with the null value. The choice between one of the techniques is completely up to your implementation considerations.

By default, JSON-B does not show properties with null values when serializing Java objects. In order to display the attributes with null values in the resulting JSON, the `@JsonNillable` annotation is used on Java classes, to tell the `jsonb` processor to use the mentioned technique, as shown in the following example:

```
@JsonbNillable
public class Movie {

    private long id;
    private String title;
    private int productionYear;

    // getters and setters

}

JsonbConfig config = new JsonbConfig().withFormatting(true);
```

```
Jsonb jsonb = JsonbBuilder.create(config);

Movie movie = new Movie();
movie.setId(15);
movie.setProductionYear(2017);

String json = jsonb.toJson(movie);
System.out.println(json);
```

In the previous example, we have created a `movie` object, initialized all its properties with data, except for the title. By running the previous example, the output will be as follows:

```
{
    "id": 15,
    "productionYear": 2017,
    "title": null
}
```

As you can see, the `title` attribute is visible in the resulting JSON, with a `null` value displayed. Without using the `@JsonbNillable` annotation, the output would be as follows:

```
{
    "id": 15,
    "productionYear": 2017
}
```

The output, as you can see, would be without even showing the existence of the `title` attribute.

Formatting dates and numbers

Dates and numbers can also be customized in the resulting JSON object. `@JsonbDateFormat` and `@JsonbNumberFormat` are used to configure dates and numbers, respectively. For `@JsonbDateFormat`, a `DateTimeFormatter` pattern is used to customize the resulting date, and for `@JsonNumberFormat`, a `DecimalFormat` pattern is used to customize the resulting number. The following example will show how to use both date and number formats:

```
public class User {

    private long id;
    private String name;
    @JsonbDateFormat("dd/MM/yyy")
```

```
            private Date birthDate;
            @JsonbDateFormat("dd/MM/yyy hh:mm a")
            private Date lastLoggedIn;
            @JsonbNumberFormat("#0.00")
            private BigDecimal averageLoggedInTime;

            // getters and setters here

        }

        JsonbConfig config = new JsonbConfig().withFormatting(true);
        Jsonb jsonb = JsonbBuilder.create(config);

        SimpleDateFormat sdfDate = new SimpleDateFormat("MM/dd/yyyy");
        SimpleDateFormat sdfTime = new SimpleDateFormat("MM/dd/yyyy hh:mm a");

        User user = new User();
        user.setId(5);
        user.setName("Abdalla Mahmoud");
        user.setBirthDate(sdfDate.parse("07/06/1988"));
        user.setLastLoggedIn(sdfTime.parse("10/06/2017 03:20 pm"));
        user.setAverageLoggedInTime(new BigDecimal("3.1562"));

        String json = jsonb.toJson(user);
        System.out.println(json);
```

The output of the previous code will be as follows:

```
{
    "averageLoggedInTime": "3.16",
    "birthDate": "05/07/1988",
    "id": 5,
    "lastLoggedIn": "06/10/2017 01:20 PM",
    "name": "Abdalla Mahmoud"
}
```

As you can see, we have used the @JsonbDateFormat annotation on the birthDate property, passing the dd/mm/yyyy pattern. This means that when serializing the object to JSON, the resulting date will be displayed as day (two digits)/month (two digits)/year (four digits). For full details of the pattern characters, you can refer to the DateTimeFormatter specification in Javadocs.

Moreover, we have used the `@JsonbNumberFormat` annotation on the `averageLoggedInTime` property, to customize the resulting number in the JSON output. By `#0.00`, we mean that the number should be displayed as integral part fractional parts rounded to two digits. For full details of the number pattern, you can refer to the `DateTimeFormatter` specification in Javadocs.

Moreover, you can set the date formatting option globally using the `jsonb` configuration object, as shown in the following example:

```
JsonbConfig config = new
JsonbConfig().withFormatting(true).withDateFormat("dd/MM/yyyy",
Locale.getDefault());
```

You can test this yourself.

Using binary

As JSON is a text-based format, associating binary data (such as file content) inside a JSON document directly is not technically feasible. Therefore, a text representation for the binary data should be used in order to be shown in the resulting JSON as an alternative to the direct bytes array.

JSON-B supports three different strategies to represent the bytes array in JSON documents:

- Binary: Using this strategy, binary data is encoded as a byte array.
- Base 64: Using this strategy, binary data is encoded using the Base64 encoding scheme as specified in RFC 4648 and RFC 2045.
- Base 64 URL: Using this strategy, binary data is encoded using the URL and Filename safe Base64 Alphabet as specified in Table 2 of RFC 4648. This is compliant with the Internet JSON (I-JSON) profile.

For example, let's define a `movie` object, with a binary array representing its thumbnail, and load the binary data from a file, as shown in the following example:

```
public class Movie {
    private long id;
    private String name;
    private byte[] thumbnail;

    // getters and setters here

}
```

```
File thumbnailFile = new File("D:\beauty_and_the_beast.jpg");
byte[] buff = new byte[(int) thumbnailFile.length()];
FileInputStream fis = new FileInputStream(thumbnailFile);
fis.read(buff);
fis.close();

Movie movie = new Movie();
movie.setId(15);
movie.setName("Beauty and the Beauty");
movie.setThumbnail(buff);

JsonbConfig jsonbConfig = new JsonbConfig();
Jsonb jsonb = JsonbBuilder.create(jsonbConfig);

String json = jsonb.toJson(movie);
System.out.println(json);
```

The output of the previous code should be as follows:

```
{"id":15,"name":"Beauty and the Beauty","thumbnail":[-1,-40,...]}
```

As you can see, a byte array is used to represent the binary data, and this is the default approach. We could also use the base 64 URL approach, as follows:

```
JsonbConfig jsonbConfig = new
JsonbConfig().withBinaryDataStrategy(BinaryDataStrategy. BASE_64_URL);
```

The output would be as follows:

```
{"id":15,"name":"Beauty and the
Beauty","thumbnail":"_9j_4AAQSkZJRgABAQEAYABgAA..."}
```

Base 64 is more standard in a web services environment and it produces less of a fingerprint than the byte mode, and is restricted to the Internet JSON (I-JSON) standard.

Summary

In this chapter, we have learned how to use the JSON-B API in parsing and generating JSON documents; this will be very useful in cases you have to some basic or advanced processing over some transformed JSON data, especially in low-level programming contexts.

In the next chapter, we will learn about one of the hottest topics in the cloud era, which is exposing RESTful web services. And as you may already know, JSON is an important player in this area—stay tuned!

Communicating with Different Systems with JMS 2.0

7

In this chapter, we are going to discuss the Java Messaging System (JMS) 2.0 API, which provides a full-featured implementation of **Message-oriented middleware** (**MOM**) in Java. If you are new to the message-oriented middleware concept, or have never used one of them before, don't worry; we are going to explain the basic concepts of messaging and JMS in the next sections.

You will learn how to use JMS 2.0 to send messages from any Java EE component to be consumed by **Message-driven beans** (**MDB**) asynchronously and concurrently. Note that the concept of messaging here is completely different from emails; emails are meant for communication between two or more persons, while messages in MOM are meant for communication between two or more software components. Emails contain some arbitrary information to be read by humans, while MOM messages are structured information to be processed by some piece of software; this information represents some function parameters that the executing part should use in processing.

You will also learn how to implement the two messaging styles of JMS, namely point-to-point and publish-subscribe. Each of them has its own characteristics, which will greatly affect your application design from the beginning and the performance factors you can consider controlling.

As a software architect, MOM (and its JMS specification in Java) is considered a classic implementation of the **event-driven architectural pattern**. In event-driven architecture, you design your software components to be loosely coupled, and they generate and react to events through channels rather than directly calling each other. In JMS, a **message** acts as the event to be generated and handled by software components, whereas a **message destination** act as the event channel to be followed. If you are new to the event-driven architectural pattern, you can search online for some good materials about it to compare it with the architectural style of JMS, which will be discussed in upcoming sections.

In the following sections, we are going to cover:

- What is Message-Oriented Middleware?
- Basic concepts of the Java Messaging System (JMS)
- Developing our first JMS application
- Using JMS resources
- Using message-driven beans

Message-Oriented Middleware

To explain the concept of MOM, let's start by having a look at a simple real-world example: suppose you want to communicate with your friend Tom to tell him about a new update about some personal news he is interested in; suppose you are going to inform him about your wedding and you want to invite him as your guest. There are two options to tell Tom about your update:

- Call him on his cell phone and invite him directly
- Send him an SMS message to invite him

What's the difference between the two options? Well, in the first option, you have to have Tom's mobile available on the network, and he should be free to answer your call and get the information from you; you will be in direct contact with Tom. In the second option, you do not have to have either Tom's mobile available or him free to answer your call. You will send the SMS message, which will be handled by what's called a message broker, which will store the message and wait until Tom's mobile is available on the network to deliver the message to him. Tom can view the message instantaneously, or maybe view it later when he is free. In this case, you are not in direct contact with Tom.

The choice between these two options is dependent a lot on your requirements for this invitation: are you really interested in having Tom's answer quickly because it will determine how many more guests you are going to invite? Is the party open and ready to host as many guests as you may get? Do you have enough time (and is it necessary) to call each one independently? Sometimes the second option is more reliable, as messages are guaranteed to be delivered, while you do not have enough time to follow up missing guests because you are busy with some other party preparation stuff.

The two options map directly in software architecture to the following two concepts:

- **Remote procedure call (RPC):** A software component calling a function in another software component remotely. In Java, the RMI API supports this model, which is a built-in feature in enterprise Java Beans (EJBs).

  The following diagram shows how the RPC technique works:

  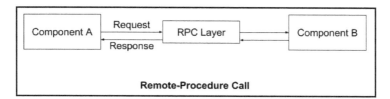

- **Message-oriented middleware (MOM):** A software component sends a message to a message broker, which delivers it to another software component remotely. In Java, the JMS API supports this model, which is integrated with the MDB API discussed later in this chapter.

  The following diagram shows how the MOM technique works:

  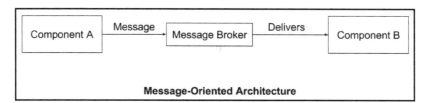

The *message broker* is a software component that receives messages from *producers* (software components that send requests), stores messages reliably, then delivers them to consumers (software components that process requests) either by order or priority; it retries the delivery in the case of consumer failure or being busy.

In the following table, we will have a technical comparison to summarize the differences between the two techniques:

RPC (Remote procedure call)	MOM (Message-oriented middleware)
Used to communicate between two software components.	Used to communicate between two software components, as well.
Synchronous—The component calls the other component directly, and waits for its response.	Asynchronous—The component calls the other component indirectly, and does not have to wait for its response.
Tightly coupled—Components depend on each other and should have awareness of and access to their interface.	Loosely coupled—The component calls an intermediate message broker, which delivers the message to the other component; it should not have awareness of or access to its actual interface.
Not reliable—If the two components are not up and free to communicate with each other, the call fails.	Reliable—If one of the two components is not up and free to communicate, the message broker guarantees that the message will be delivered once the destination is up and capable of serving more messages.
Complex scalability—Needs vertical scaling (more nodes in a cluster, for example) to support a heavy load of concurrent requests.	Simple scalability—Horizontal scaling can be applied to process a heavy load of messages by simply keeping and processing them by a queue.

So, when to choose to use MOM over RPC? If one of the following circumstances exists, then there is a high probability that you are in need of MOM:

- **Asynchronous communication requirements:** If the business logic supports resuming the original operation without caring about the execution of other operations, then here we can go with MOM. For example, in a cinema booking application, reserving a cinema ticket is dependent on the online payment process to be completed successfully, so a call to the payment service should be performed synchronously using RCP (EJBs in the context of Java EE). But after payment, the process of sending an SMS and/or email confirmation to the user, informing the analytics module about the new reservation, or passing the information to the accounting auditor, operations don't usually need to be completed before telling the user that his/her reservation is done. Hence, a call to the aforementioned modules could be performed asynchronously using MOM (JMS in the context of Java EE).

- **Loose coupling:** If there is a possibility that other services may be down, and this should not affect the availability of the original service, then we can go with MOM. For example, the mail server may be down at the time of user reservation, but this should not stop the user reservation process, and it's acceptable that the message may have some delay in delivery to the user. In this case, a direct call to the messaging service is not a good idea, and it's more reliable to use a message broker instead.
- **Performance requirements:** You can use MOM to enhance your overall system performance and decrease the operational time for business operations by allowing sub-activities to be executed asynchronously and concurrently.

Java Messaging System (JMS)

As we mentioned earlier, JMS is the Java standard API for implementing message-oriented middleware. Any typical Java EE application server (Glassfish, Wildfly, WebLogic, and so on) will have its own implementation for this API. In other words, you don't care, as a Java EE application developer, about the actual implementation used within an application server, and you will be focusing more on API concepts.

In the next section, we are going to discuss the architecture and the constituent parts of a typical JMS application.

Architecture

JMS is a platform-neutral Java API, which means that it can be used within the context of any Java SE application and is not limited to Java EE. In the following sections, we are going to explain the different parts that make up a typical JMS application, but with a focus on JMS usage from the perspective of Java EE.

JMS provider

An implementation of the JMS API, always bundled with any Java EE application server. However, as mentioned earlier, you can use an independent implementation within a Java SE application.

JMS clients

Software components that communicate with each other. There are two types of JMS client:

- **Producers:** Software components that send messages
- **Consumers:** Software components that receive messages and process them by doing the corresponding action

In JMS, you can nearly write a client consuming messages, inside any type of Java classes—POJOs, sessions beans, servlets, and so on. However, in the Java EE platform specifically, message-driven beans are the standard way to implement JMS clients, as they integrate well with the application server and other services it provides.

Note that consuming JMS messages in Java SE, or even non-Java languages, is also possible; however, those topics are beyond the scope of this book.

Messages

Messages are the main concern of JMS; they are objects passed from some producer to one or more consumers. A message contains information that is used by the consumer to determine which action to perform, and the required parameters to use. In JMS, there are different types of message, as listed in the following table:

Message Type	Description
TextMessage	A payload of a string value.
MapMessage	A payload of a Java map to a set of pairs; a string value is used as a key, and any other Java primitive value (including strings and byte arrays) can be used as a value for each key. Note that the order of keys is not guaranteed, like in any Java map.
BytesMessage	A payload of arbitrary bytes.
StreamMessage	A payload of Java primitive values, read and written sequentially.
ObjectMessage	A payload of Java Serializable objects.
Message	A message with headers and properties only, without a payload.

Administered objects

JMS administered objects are objects configured to be used by JMS clients. There are two kinds of administered objects that you should use within any JMS application:

- **Connection Factories:** Objects used by JMS clients to establish a connection with a JMS provider fed with the required connection configuration prepared by the system administrator.
- **Destinations:** A destination is an object used by JMS client to specify the target component(s) that should be receiving this message. Two destination types are available in JMS:
  - **Queue** (used in the point-to-point messaging style)
  - **Topic** (used in the publish-subscribe messaging style)

These two messaging styles will be discussed in the next section.

Messaging styles

In JMS, two message styles are available to choose from when deciding to use a message-oriented architecture. Each style can address a different business problem, while providing nearly the same messaging interface.

Point-to-point style

In point-to-point messaging (P2P for short), the message broker maintains a **destination queue** with an ID. When a producer sends a message targeting a specific queue by ID, the broker enqueues the message in this queue. When a consumer asks to receive and process a new message from this queue, the message broker will dequeue a single message in a first-in-first-out manner and deliver it to this producer.

Queues in messaging can provide scaling capabilities with low costs, as this model supports processing a large queue with messages using a limited number of concurrent consumers. A large number of messages can be waiting in a queue to be served once a single consumer is free to accept more messages.

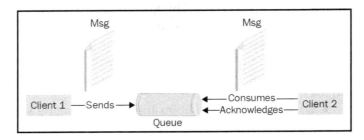

Publish-subscribe

In the publish-subscribe messaging style, the message broker maintains a destination topic with an ID. One or more interested consumers will subscribe to this topic. When a producer sends a message to this topic, all interested (subscribed) consumers will be notified with the new message.

Topics in messaging can provide multiple consumers for a single message; this allows distributing the message to different consumers concurrently, as each consumer is interested in performing a single kind of post-processing action, according to the message. JMS states that only messages sent after subscription to this topic will be delivered to the consumer, with no delivery of messages sent before this subscription or in the case of inactivity by the consumer. However, JMS can extend this concept using durable subscriptions, which also deliver messages sent during inactivity:

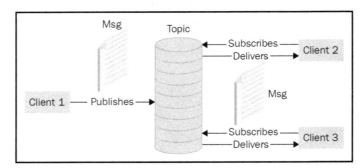

First JMS application

In the following sections, we are going to show how to send a text message from a servlet (acting as a producer) to a consumer (an MDB) using a topic destination.

Creating administered objects

As mention earlier, two administered objects are needed by JMS clients to start exchanging messages—destinations and connection factories. In this section, we are going to create those two administered objects to be used in our basic JMS example, from the GlassFish administration console. However, in a later section, we are going to show how can you define those administered objects from inside your application itself, using simple annotations.

Creating a destination

Log in to your GlassFish administration console by browsing to `http://localhost:9322` (change the port to the one bound to your GlassFish administration HTTP listener if necessary):

1. From the **Common Tasks** pane, navigate to **Resources** | **JMS Resources** | **Destination Resources**
2. Click **New**
3. In `JNDI Name`, write `jms/ticketsReservationTopic`
4. In **Physical Destination Name**, write `ticketsReservationTopic`
5. In **Resource Type**, leave it as `javax.jms.Topic`
6. Click **OK**

Creating a connection factory

Using the same GlassFish administration console:

1. From the **Common Tasks** pane, navigate to **Resources** | **JMS Resources** | **Connection Factories**
2. Click **New**
3. In **JNDI Name**, write `jms/ticketsReservationFactory`

4. In **Resource Type**, leave it as `javax.jms.TopicConnectionFactory`
5. Click **OK**:

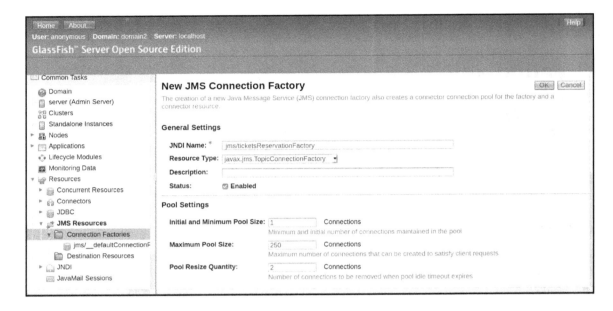

Creating the producer

In this simple example, we will use a servlet to send a message to the `ticketsReservationTopic` we just created in the previous section.

We will define a servlet, `TicketReservationServlet`, which will be used to send a message to this destination topic. To send a message, we need to look up two resources: the connection factory and the destination. We will use the dependency injection technique to look them up using the `@Resource` annotation, as shown in the following example:

```
@WebServlet(urlPatterns = "/tickets/reserve")
public class TicketReservationServlet extends HttpServlet {

    @Resource(lookup = "jms/ticketsReservationFactory")
    private ConnectionFactory connectionFactory;

    @Resource(lookup = "jms/ticketsReservationTopic")
    private Topic topic;

    @Override
```

```
        protected void doGet(HttpServletRequest req, HttpServletResponse resp)
throws ServletException, IOException {
        try {
            // create a JMS context object
JMSContext context = connectionFactory.createContext();
            // create JMS producer object from this context
            JMSProducer producer = context.createProducer();
            // create a JMS text message from this context
            TextMessage textMessage = context.createTextMessage();
            textMessage.setText("Hello JMS!");
            // send the text message
            producer.send(topic, textMessage);
            resp.getOutputStream().println("Message sent successfully!");
        } catch (Exception ex) {
            ex.printStackTrace();
        }
    }

}
```

As you see, we have introduced two member variables—connectionFactory and a topic
with @Resource annotations to inject the resources defined in the GlassFish administration
console. These are the JM-administered objects needed to perform the communication.
Then, upon a GET request, we are going to create a JMSContext object from this connection
factory using this line:

```
JMSContext context = connectionFactory.createContext();
```

The JMSContext object holds two primary JMS objects: a connection and a session. A
connection is a TCP connection with the message broker, and the session is a single-
threaded channel to send messages over this connection. The createContext() object is
used to create both a connection (maybe pooled) and a session within this connection. You
use the JMSContext object to create a JMSProducer object, which is in turn used to
actually send JMS messages to a specific destination. We have created the JMSProducer
object in this line:

```
JMSProducer producer = context.createProducer();
```

Then, we have used the JMSContext object to create a text message, fed with context, with
these two lines:

```
TextMessage textMessage = context.createTextMessage();
textMessage.setText("First message");
```

And finally, we send the message to our destination topic with this line:

```
producer.send(topic, textMessage);
```

Creating the consumer

As mentioned earlier, the consumer in JMS can be any object or component; however, it's typically an MDB in Java EE. We will discuss message-driven beans in a separate section, but we are going to create a simple one now for the purpose of our demonstration example:

```
@MessageDriven(activationConfig = {
    @ActivationConfigProperty(propertyName = "destinationLookup",
            propertyValue = "jms/ticketsReservationTopic")
    ,
    @ActivationConfigProperty(propertyName = "destinationType",
            propertyValue = "javax.jms.Topic")
})
public class ReservationBean implements MessageListener {

    @Override
    public void onMessage(Message msg) {
        try {
            System.out.println("********* " + ((TextMessage)
msg).getText());
        } catch (JMSException ex) {
            ex.printStackTrace();
        }
    }

}
```

As you see, we have defined a message-driven bean component by annotating our class with the @MessageDriven annotation, where we have specified two activation configuration properties:

1. destinationLookup: The JNDI name of the topic this bean should be listening to
2. destinationType: The type of this destination, which is a topic in our example

Then we have implemented the MessageListener interface (discussed in more detail later), overriding onMessage, where we are going to be notified about new incoming messages. Upon receiving a message, we cast the message type to its actual implementation, which is TextMessage in our example, printing its contents to the console of the application server.

Now, to test this example, call the servlet created in the previous section by simply using the browser to call `/tickets/reserve`, and you should be seeing the application server's console display this:

```
********* Hello JMS!
```

This way, we have sent and received our JMS message.

Using JMS resources with annotations

In the previous example, we showed how to create JMS resources using the GlassFish administration console. This is very useful when you need to register factories and destinations that work across different applications. However, if your JMS resources are local to your application, that is, no other applications are going to communicate with you on a JMS channel, it's much simpler to use annotations to define application-specific JMS resources. Those annotations can be used on any Java EE component class.

Creating connection factories

In order to create a destination resource, you can use the `@JMSDestinationDefinition` annotation as follows:

```
@JMSConnectionFactoryDefinition(
        name = "java:app/jms/MyConnectionFactory"
)
```

You can also configure some properties of your connection factory; for example, you can set the minimum and maximum pool size for this connection factory, as follows:

```
@JMSConnectionFactoryDefinition(
        name = "java:app/jms/MyConnectionFactory",
        minPoolSize = 5,
        maxPoolSize = 50
)
```

You can also define more than one destination on the same class by using the `@JMSConnectionFactoryDefinitions` annotation, passing it an array of `@JMSConnectionFactoryDefinition` annotations as shown in the previous example, like so:

```
@JMSConnectionFactoryDefinitions({
    @JMSConnectionFactoryDefinition(
```

```
                  name = "java:app/jms/MyConnectionFactory1"
        )
        ,
        @JMSConnectionFactoryDefinition(
                  name = "java:app/jms/MyConnectionFactory2"
        )
})
```

Creating destinations

In order to create a destination resource, you can use the `@JMSDestinationDefinition` annotation, as follows:

```
@JMSDestinationDefinition(
        name = "java:app/jms/myQueue",
        interfaceName = "javax.jms.Queue",
        destinationName = "myQueue"
)
```

The attributes shown are the minimum required to define your destination:

`name`: The JNDI name of the resource.

`interfaceName`: The name of the interface to use for this destination. The value may be `javax.jms.Queue` or `javax.jms.Topic`.

`destinationName`: The physical name of the destination; your choice.

You can also define more than one destination on the same class by using the `@JMSDestinationDefinitions` annotation, passing it an array of `@JMSDestinationDefinition` annotations as shown in the previous example, as follows:

```
@JMSDestinationDefinitions({
    @JMSDestinationDefinition(
            name = "java:app/jms/myQueue1",
            interfaceName = "javax.jms.Queue",
            destinationName = "myQueue1"
    )
    ,@JMSDestinationDefinition(
            name = "java:app/jms/myQueue2",
            interfaceName = "javax.jms.Queue",
            destinationName = "myQueue2"
    )
})
```

Injecting connection factories

In order to inject a JMS connection factory into another Java EE component, you can simply use the `@Resource` annotation, passing the lookup attribute, the JNDI name of your connection factory, as follows:

```
@Resource(lookup = "java:app/jms/MyConnectionFactory")
private ConnectionFactory myConnectionFactory;
```

You will then have to create a `JMSContext` object from this factory to send your messages, as follows:

```
JMSContext context = myConnectionFactory.createContext();
context.createProducer().send(queue, "Hello JMS!");
```

However, a better approach exists—inject a `JMSContext` object directly by using the `@Inject` and `@JMSConnectionFactory` annotations together, as follows:

```
@Inject
@JMSConnectionFactory("java:app/jms/MyConnectionFactory")
private JMSContext context;
```

This way, you can use the context object directly within your EE component. This is a more commonly used approach in Java EE applications.

Injecting destinations

In order to inject a JMS destination into another Java EE component, you can also use the `@Resource` annotation as shown in the previous example:

```
@Resource(lookup = "java:app/jms/myQueue")
private Queue queue;
```

Note that if the destination type is `Topic`, you will have to use `Topic` as the type of your introduced variable.

Putting them all together

In the following example, we will show how to define JMS-administered objects using annotations, then how to send and receive messages using those objects. We will start by defining a message-driven bean, with the @JMSDestinationDefinition and @JMSConnectionFactoryDefinition annotations, to introduce a destination queue and connection factory, as follows:

```
@JMSDestinationDefinition(
        name = "java:app/jms/myQueue",
        interfaceName = "javax.jms.Queue",
        destinationName = "myQueue"
)
@JMSConnectionFactoryDefinition(
        name = "java:app/jms/MyConnectionFactory"
)
@MessageDriven(activationConfig = {
    @ActivationConfigProperty(propertyName = "destinationLookup",
propertyValue = "java:app/jms/myQueue")
    ,
    @ActivationConfigProperty(propertyName = "destinationType",
propertyValue = "javax.jms.Queue")
})
public class ClientMDB implements MessageListener {

    @Override
    public void onMessage(Message msg) {
        try {
            System.out.println("Received: " + ((TextMessage)
msg).getText());
        } catch (JMSException ex) {
            ex.printStackTrace();
        }
    }

}
```

We have also configured our message-driven bean to use those resources by their JNDI name. Now, we will define a ClientServlet, which will send a message to this destination, as follows:

```
@WebServlet(urlPatterns = "/test")
public class ClientServlet extends HttpServlet {

    @Inject
    @JMSConnectionFactory("java:app/jms/MyConnectionFactory")
```

```
    private JMSContext context;

    @Resource(lookup = "java:app/jms/myQueue")
    private Queue queue;

    @Override
    protected void doGet(HttpServletRequest req, HttpServletResponse resp)
throws ServletException, IOException {
        context.createProducer().send(queue, "Hello JMS!");
    }

}
```

We have used the @Inject annotation to inject a JMS context object (which represents a connection and a session within a JMS broker), specifying the connection factory to use with the @JMSConnectionFactory annotation, and passing its JNDI name. We have used the @Resource annotation to inject the destination resource, also bypassing its JNDI name. Then, via a get request to this servlet, we used the context object to create a producer to send a text message to this queue, in this line:

```
context.createProducer().send(queue, "Hello JMS!");
```

Test the example by requesting /test using your web browser; the message-driven bean should receive the message and print it to your GlassFish console:

Received: Hello JMS!

Message-Driven Beans

A message-driven bean (MDB) is an enterprise bean that is used in Java EE to receive and process messages asynchronously, whatever the messaging style used: point-to-point or publish-subscribe. Any other component—servlets; EJBs; other MDBs; or another Java EE, SE, or non-Java application—can send messages to be processed by message-driven beans. Message-driven beans act as the message listener in JMS.

Message-driven beans are similar to stateful session beans in that:

- They maintain no conversational state (stateless).
- All instances of message-driven beans are equal. Therefore, the application server can maintain a pool of them to serve many requests (messages) concurrently.

- A single instance of a message-driven bean can serve requests (messages) from different clients.

However, message-driven beans differ from session beans in that:

- They have no standard interface to access.
- They are indirectly accessible by sending message objects to the JMS destination those message-driven beans are registered to.
- The call happens asynchronously.

Creating a message-driven bean

Message-driven beans should implement the `MessageListener` interface. The interface includes one abstract method—`onMessage(Message msg)`. The bean should override this method, cast the `Message` parameter to the appropriate message type, then do whatever action it should perform with the message contents. The following code snippet shows the general structure of a message-driven bean:

```
public class ClientMDB implements MessageListener {

    @Override
    public void onMessage(Message msg) {
        // cast message and process it here
    }

}
```

The message-driven bean should be annotated with the `@MessageDriven` annotation, passing the `activationConfig` value, which is an array of configuration properties that specify how the message-driven bean works, for example:

```
@MessageDriven(activationConfig = {
    @ActivationConfigProperty(propertyName = "destinationLookup",
propertyValue = "java:app/jms/myQueue")
    ,
    @ActivationConfigProperty(propertyName = "destinationType",
propertyValue = "javax.jms.Queue")
})
public class ClientMDB implements MessageListener {

    . . . .

}
```

In this example, we have used an array of `@ActivationConfigProperty` as the activation configuration for the message-driven beans. The two properties `destinationLookup` and `destionationType` define the JNDI name and the type of the destination this bean should be listening to.

Sending and receiving messages

Messages are objects that hold information to be processed by a message listener or a message-driven bean. Different types of message exist to support the different types of payload you will be sending to the interested components. In the following sections, we are going to show how to send and receive the following types of message—text, map, and object messages. You can refer to the documentation to examine and use other types of message, although I'm sure you will get this knowledge by only using your IDE's auto-complete.

Text messages

Text messages hold strings. You create a text message by calling the `createTextMessage` method of the JMS context object, passing it some string content, as shown in the following example:

```
TextMessage textMessage = context.createTextMessage("some text");
context.createProducer().send(queue, textMessage);
```

When receiving this message, the message reference should be cast to `TextMessage`; then, retrieve the text content by calling the `getText()` method, as follows:

```
....
@Override
public void onMessage(Message msg) {
    try {
        // cast to text message
        TextMessage message = (TextMessage) msg;
        // process
        System.out.println(message.getText());
    } catch (JMSException ex) {
        ex.printStackTrace();
    }
}
....
```

This way, we can process the text content of our received message.

Map messages

Map messages are used to compose a more complex message with many fields of different basic types. They are very similar to Java maps included in the collection interface, with the following conditions:

- Keys are of type string
- Values are of primitive types, Strings, byte arrays, or serializable objects

Also, to put values in map messages, the classic put method is absent here. The methods `setInt`, `setLong`, `setObject`, and others are used to add/update new key value pairs to your map message.

The following example shows how can we create and feed a map message:

```
// create a map message
MapMessage mapMessage = context.createMapMessage();

// put values
mapMessage.setString("name", "foo");
mapMessage.setInt("count", 50);

// send it
context.createProducer().send(queue, mapMessage);
```

In your message-driven bean, you should cast your message to a `MapMessage` object, then use the methods `getString`, `getInt`, and so on to retrieve different values fed into this map using their corresponding keys, as shown in the following example:

```
....
@Override
public void onMessage(Message msg) {
    try {
        // cast to map message
        MapMessage message = (MapMessage) msg;
        // read values and process them
        System.out.println(message.getString("name"));
        System.out.println(message.getInt("count"));
    } catch (JMSException ex) {
        ex.printStackTrace();
    }
}
....
```

This way, we can process all values included in the received map message.

Object messages

Object messages are a more advanced type of message and support sending complex Java objects as the content of your messages. One main condition that should be met on your content object is that they should be `Serializable`. The JMS broker will use Java Serialization to serialize/deserialize exchanging objects. For example, suppose we are going to send a payment information object with some important payment details. We should define our class to implement the `Serializable` interface, as shown in the following example:

```java
public class PaymentInfo implements Serializable{
    private int id;
    private BigDecimal amount;

    public int getId() {
        return id;
    }

    public void setId(int id) {
        this.id = id;
    }

    public BigDecimal getAmount() {
        return amount;
    }

    public void setAmount(BigDecimal amount) {
        this.amount = amount;
    }
}
```

Then we would create an object message and send some payment information, as shown in the following example:

```java
// create object content
PaymentInfo paymentInfo = new PaymentInfo();
paymentInfo.setId(1005);
paymentInfo.setAmount(new BigDecimal("185.1"));

// create an object message instance, passing it the content
ObjectMessage objectMessage = context.createObjectMessage();
objectMessage.setObject(paymentInfo);

// send it
context.createProducer().send(queue, objectMessage);
```

When consuming the message in your message-driven bean, you should cast the message to the `ObjectMessage` type, retrieve it, and cast the object to the `PaymentInfo` type, as shown in the following example:

```
    ....
    @Override
    public void onMessage(Message msg) {
        try {
            // cast to object message
            ObjectMessage message = (ObjectMessage) msg;

            // cast message content to the appropriate object
            PaymentInfo paymentInfo = (PaymentInfo) message.getObject();

            // read values and process them
            System.out.println("*** New Payment ***");
            System.out.println("Payment ID: " + paymentInfo.getId());
            System.out.println("Payment Amount: " +
paymentInfo.getAmount());

        } catch (JMSException ex) {
            ex.printStackTrace();
        }
    }
    ....
```

We then restored the message content to a `PaymentInfo` instance, and this way we can retrieve and process every important detail in this object.

Summary

In this chapter, we introduced the idea of message-oriented middleware and its parent pattern (event-driven architecture). Also, we have discussed in some detail the basic concepts of message-oriented middleware, JMS APIs, and message-driven beans, with some basic examples. There's more to learn about these, for sure. You can refer to the official documentation for more complicated and advanced usage scenarios.

In the next chapter, we are going to explain another form of communication: software-human communication. We are going to learn how to programmatically send emails using the JavaMail APIs and Gmail.

Sending Mails with JavaMail 1.6

8

In any enterprise application, sending emails is a very common action to perform during many user interactions with your application. Some example use cases of sending email within your enterprise application include:

- Sending confirmation and welcoming emails upon user registration
- Sending password reset links to users who forget their passwords
- Sending an email notifying users about different events or announcements they may be interested in

The Java Mail API provides Java standard interfaces used to access email features within your enterprise application. You can use it both to send mails to some recipients, and access (retrieve) you email messages from your inbox.

In the next sections, we are going to cover:

- A brief introduction to the main mailing protocols
- Programmatically sending plain text and HTML emails
- Specifying the To, CC, and BCC fields in mails
- Attaching files to your emails

Note that retrieving emails from your Inbox is beyond the scope of this chapter.

Explaining mail protocols

Before delving into how to send emails via the Java Mail API, let's first gain an awareness of the different web protocols related to mailing systems. The three popular protocols used are POP3, IMAP, and SMTP. Both POP3 and IMAP are used to retrieve emails from a mail server, while the SMTP protocol is used to send (deliver) messages.

POP3 and IMAP

POP3 is a protocol used to access an email from the server, download new emails to the client, then delete the emails from the server. In POP3, if you have checked your emails from one device then tried to access them again from another device, you will find that your emails are no longer available, as they were deleted upon accessing them from the first device.

IMAP is also another email access protocol. Unlike POP3, it does not delete original emails from the server, and therefore is suitable for allowing email access from different devices, as your emails are always there on the server. Accordingly, it's the most widely used protocol for accessing email.

SMTP

The **Simple Mail Transfer Protocol** (**SMTP**) for short, is a plain text protocol used to transmit emails over the internet. SMTP is different to both POP3 and IMAP in that this protocol is used only for sending (relaying) and receiving emails on email server levels only. Client-level applications use either POP3 or IMAP to access email. The main purpose of the SMTP protocol is as simple as this—receive emails from clients, then route them to their destination servers.

SMTP connections are commonly secured by **Transport Layer Security** (**TLS**), which is very similar to **Secure Socket Layer** (**SSL**) used in HTTPs. Moreover, most modern SMTP relays require client authentication before receiving an email from the client and routing it to its destination.

Sending an email

In the following example, we are going to send a plain text email to a recipient. As shown in the previous section, we will need to have an SMTP server available to enable us to send emails to the desired recipients. In this example and the next ones, we will use Gmail as our SMTP relay server.

 Note: I highly recommend registering a new email address for testing purposes, and not using your current main one. This is because you may somehow forget your own credentials are inside the code, and they might be viewed by someone later. Moreover, if you have not enabled two-way authentication, it's better to quickly enable this mode now!

Create a test method space to run your example, either in a servlet or a JAX-RS service, then write the following code inside it:

```
// recipient mail: replace by your main email:
String to = "****@gmail.com";

// sender mail and credentials: replace by your testing email:
String from = "****@gmail.com";
final String username = "****@gmail.com";
final String password = "****";

// the host of Google's SMTP service:
String host = "smtp.gmail.com";

// mail properties object
Properties props = new Properties();
// enable use authentication
props.put("mail.smtp.auth", "true");
// enable encrypted connection
props.put("mail.smtp.starttls.enable", "true");
// setting host and port
props.put("mail.smtp.host", host);
props.put("mail.smtp.port", "587");

// creating a mail session
Session session = Session.getInstance(props,
        new javax.mail.Authenticator() {
    protected PasswordAuthentication getPasswordAuthentication() {
        return new PasswordAuthentication(username, password);
    }
});

try {
```

```
        // creating a message object
        Message message = new MimeMessage(session);
        // filling mail attributes
        message.setFrom(new InternetAddress(from));
        message.setRecipients(Message.RecipientType.TO,
                InternetAddress.parse(to));
        message.setSubject("Mail Subject");
        message.setText("Mail body...");
        //sending the mail
        Transport.send(message);

        System.out.println("Sent message successfully!");

    } catch (MessagingException e) {
        System.out.println("Error sending mail!");
        e.printStackTrace();
    }
```

Now, call the test servlet/service you implemented your code snippet inside, and you will get the email delivered to your defined recipient!

As you can see, we have created a `properties` object, holding all the configuration properties required to send email using Gmail's SMTP. Next, we have created an email session object, passing two values to its constructor—this `properties` object and an instance of the `Authenticator` object (implemented as an anonymous inner class), which returns an instance of the `PasswordAuthenticator` object and actually holds the username and password for the client, are passed as arguments to its constructor. After that, we have created an instance of the `MimeMessage` object, passing our session to its constructor, in order to start composing our mail. Later, we have set the mail information (the sender, the recipients, the subject, and the text). Finally, we have called the send message from the `Transport` class, passing the MIME message object, which will actually send our final composed email.

In the following table, we summarize the set of classes used in the previous example:

Class	Description
Session	An instance of this class represents a mail session, which maintains email connection information and is used to create and send emails.
Authenticator	An abstract class used by applications to provide the authentication methodology implementation used to actually connect to the email server. This class should be implemented to return the PasswordAuthentication object that holds the username and password used to authenticate with the email server.
PasswordAuthentication	An instance of this class holds the credentials used to access email by a specific session object, using the username/password credentials model.
Message	An abstract class represents whose actual implementations represent email messages. A message holds a set of attributes (recipient, subject, and so on) together with the message content (body).
MimeMessage	An instance of this class represents a MIME-style email message, which is the mainstream standard to send emails in the web world.
Transport	This class is used to actually send email messages, using the static send method.

Sending an HTML email message

Sometimes you need to include rich content in your mail body, such as formatted text and images. You can use HTML instead of plain text as the body of your email. The following example alters the previous one to do this using the Java Mail API:

```
    . . . .
    Message message = new MimeMessage(session);
    // filling mail attributes
    message.setFrom(new InternetAddress(from));
    message.setRecipients(Message.RecipientType.TO,
            InternetAddress.parse(to));
    message.setSubject("Mail Subject");
    message.setContent("<html>Hello <b>World</b></html>",
  "text/html; charset=utf-8");
    . . . .
```

As you can see, we have used the `setContent` method of the message object, rather than the `setText` method. `setContent` has been passed two parameters:

- The content object, which is a string with HTML content
- The MIME type of the object, which is `text/html`. By using `text/html` as the MIME type, any email client will identify this message as HTML, and will render it with the associated format according to the HTML specification

The `setContent()` method will be used to include more advanced content, such as multi-part message objects that include one or more attachments of binary files, as will be shown in the next section.

Setting To, CC, and BCC fields

In the following example, we are going to show how to include the To, CC, and BCC fields in our email messages:

```
. . . .
String[] arrTo = {};
String[] arrCC = {};
String[] arrBCC = {};

// setting to
for (String to : arrTo) {
    message.addRecipient(Message.RecipientType.TO, new
InternetAddress(to));
}

// setting cc
for (String cc : arrCC) {
    message.addRecipient(Message.RecipientType.CC, new
InternetAddress(cc));
}

// setting bbc
for (String bcc : arrBCC) {
    message.addRecipient(Message.RecipientType.BCC, new
InternetAddress(bcc));
}
. . . .
```

As you see, we have used the `addRecipient` method to include multiple recipients to our email message, where the first parameter denotes whether this recipient is either To, CC, or BCC by using the `Message.RecipientType.*` constant.

Sending an email with attachments

In the following example, we are going to show how to send an email message with an attachment. This is done by using what's called a multi-part message, which is an extension to the mail protocol to include messages with different parts, where one or more of them are file parts with binary data, rather than regular text. The concept of multi-part in the web is very popular in associating files with a specific request. Remember that we have used multi-part-style requests in the JAX-RS chapter, to upload a file to a RESTful service:

```
        ....
Message message = new MimeMessage(session);

// filling mail attributes
message.setFrom(new InternetAddress(from));
message.setRecipients(Message.RecipientType.TO,
        InternetAddress.parse(to));
message.setSubject("Mail Subject");

// creeate a multipart content object
Multipart multipart = MimeMultipart();
// create a message part for mail body
BodyPart messageBodyPart = new MimeBodyPart();

// set the message body in this part
messageBodyPart.setText("This is message body");

// add the part to the content
multipart.addBodyPart(messageBodyPart);

// create another part for the mail attachment
messageBodyPart = new MimeBodyPart();
// add the file to this part
String filename = "/path/to/file.ext"; // change with your real path
DataSource source = new FileDataSource(filename);
messageBodyPart.setDataHandler(new DataHandler(source));
messageBodyPart.setFileName("image.jpg");
multipart.addBodyPart(messageBodyPart);

// set the message content to include all the parts
message.setContent(multipart);
```

```
// sending the mail
Transport.send(message);
```

. . . .

In this example, we have used an instance of the `MimeMultipart` class as the content of the message, rather than a string instance with plain text. The `MimeMultipart` instance has been associated with two instances of the `MimeBodyPart` class. The first instance contains the text of the body of the message, whereas the second one contains the file contents of our attachment. The first part has been associated with plain text by using the `setText` method of the `MimeBodyPart` class. The second part has been associated with a binary file by using the `setDataHandler` method, passing an instance of a `DataHandler` class that encapsulates a data source referring to some file in your local filesystem. The filename itself is set using the `setFileName` method. And finally, we actually sent the email by using the `send` method of the `Transport` class.

The following table summarizes the key classes used in the previous code excerpt:

Class	Description
`Multipart`	A `multipart` object acts as a container that holds multiple body parts. `Multipart` provides methods to retrieve and set its subparts. This class is abstract, and its primary implementation is the `MimeMultipart` class shown in the next section.
`MimeMultipart`	The `MimeMultipart` class is an implementation of the abstract `Multipart` class that uses MIME conventions for the multipart data.
`BodyPart`	This class models a `Part` that is contained within a `Multipart`. This is an abstract class. Subclasses provide actual implementations.
`MimeBodyPart`	This class represents a MIME body part. It implements the `BodyPart` abstract class and the `MimePart` interface. `MimeBodyPart`s are contained in `MimeMultipart` objects.

Summary

In this chapter, we learned to use the Java Mail API to send emails using a Gmail account. We learned how to send an email message with plain text or with rich HTML. We also learned how to include To, CC, and BCC recipient fields in our email message. And finally, we learned how to include attachments within our email message.

In the next chapter, we are going to learn how to secure our enterprise application with the newly introduced Java Security API 1.0, which was introduced in the Java EE 8 specification for the first time.

Securing an Application with Java Security 1.0

9

Security is the most important aspect of any middleware solution in the cloud era. By security, we mean authentication and authorization features found in nearly any kind of software solution. Any of your users should log in to identify themselves before delving into your system, and also should be authorized to access whatever resources they are requesting from your system.

Since the beginning of Java EE, security APIs (namely JACC and JASPIC) have always been there. However, over time, those APIs got more complex and became just not flexible enough to support the required features of modern security APIs in an easy and standard manner. Therefore, in Java EE 8, a new security API has been introduced (without elimination of the mentioned legacy APIs) to overcome the problems mentioned earlier.

In this chapter, we're going to explore the fundamentals of the new security API by learning about the following:

- What are the concepts and terminology related to the new security API?
- How to get started with the API by creating a simple login example?
- What are identity stores and their types?
- How to use the authentication context object?
- How to use authentication mechanism objects?

Terminology

In this section, we're going to list and explain the different concepts and terminology required to understand how the new security API works, and we'll get ready for moving on with the code of this new API.

Authentication mechanism

An authentication mechanism is a way used to obtain a username and password from the user, to be processed later by the Java Security API.

Different authentication mechanisms may be used, including the following:

- **HTTP Basic Authentication**: The built-in browser authentication methodology, where the browser displays an internal login dialog for the user upon trying to request access on some protected resource in our application
- **Form-Based Authentication**: The most popular way of authenticating users in web applications, where we use a custom- created HTML form to input claimed user credentials from our user

Caller

The user that's making a request to our application. This caller is our candidate for authentication and authorization, before accessing our protected resources.

Caller principal

A caller principal is an object that's used to represent the caller, which only holds the associated username.

Identity store

A component acts as a **DAO** (**Data Access Object**) for accessing user information, including their usernames, passwords, and associated roles. Many identity store types are introduced in the new security API, including the following:

- Database identity store: An object that maps users in a database table to the context of the security API.
- LDAP identity store: An object that maps users in an LDAP server.
- Custom identity store: A custom defined object where you can implement your own methodology for retrieving user information. It may be useful in cases where user information is obtained in a non-standard way, such as using special third-party web services and in cases of non-ODBC databases.

Basic login example

In this section, we're going to write a simple example to show how things work in the new security API. Our example will be about a web page (servlet) that should be secured. A user should log in by providing a valid username and a password to be able to access the mentioned page.

In the new security API, this will be done as follows:

1. Creating a web page to protect
2. Mentioning who are allowed to access the web page
3. Defining users and associated roles in a database
4. Mapping security configuration to the user database

Creating a web page to protect

Let's start by creating a simple servlet that just welcomes the user to their home:

```
@WebServlet("/home")
public class HomeServlet extends HttpServlet {

    @Override
    protected void doGet(HttpServletRequest req, HttpServletResponse resp)
            throws ServletException, IOException {
        resp.getOutputStream().println("Welcome to your home!");
    }
}
```

Now, just try to access the resource by browsing /sec/home. You should get the following result:

```
Welcome to your home!
```

As you can see, you can access your resources without a problem. Seems natural, doesn't it?

Mentioning who's allowed to access the web page

In this step, we're going to use the @ServletSecurity annotation. The annotation is used to define the roles allowed to access the resource, as follows:

```
@WebServlet("/home")
@ServletSecurity(@HttpConstraint(rolesAllowed = "user"))
public class HomeServlet extends HttpServlet {
    ...
}
```

As you can see, we've just passed @HttpConstraint to the @ServletSecurity annotation. This annotation is used within the @ServletSecurity annotation to represent the security constraints to be applied to all HTTP protocol methods (GET, POST, and so on). The rolesAllowed attribute is used to specify roles that should have access on this resource. This role will be defined in a later section.

For now, let's try to understand what we've just written. Run the application, browse /home, and you should get the default browser authentication dialog, as shown in the following screenshot:

But what username and password should you use? You'll need to define your users and associated roles first before we can proceed, which will be shown in the next step.

Defining users and associated roles in a database

If you're already familiar with similar security frameworks, you should have some sort of user/roles storage to be used within your application. This storage can be of one or more different types, including database store, LDAP store, file store, or any other custom stores.

In this example, we're going to use a database to store all our users and passwords for later authentication. So, let's start by creating a users table within your favorite database management system. We will use mysql in our example.

With your favorite mysql client, create a database called sec, and then create the users table by executing the following command:

```
CREATE TABLE users
(
    username varchar(256) PRIMARY KEY,
    password varchar(256),
    ugroup varchar(256)
);
```

As you can see, we've just created a table with three columns: username, password, and group. The group column will be representing the associated role to the user in the row.

Note that in a real-world scenario, a user may be associated with multiple roles, which requires some sort of one-to-many representation. For the sake of simplicity, we've used a many-to-one relationship instead.

Now, let's insert an arbitrary user to be used within our application by executing the following SQL command:

```
INSERT INTO users (username, password, ugroup)
VALUES ('Tom', 'tomtom', 'user')
```

As you can see, we've just created a user called Tom, with password tomtom, and associated him with the group user.

Mapping security configuration to the user database

Now, in order to be able to access our database within our example, we'll need to create a data source first. In your `resources` folder, create a `glassfish-resources.xml` file with the following content:

```xml
<?xml version="1.0" encoding="UTF-8"?>
<resources>
    <jdbc-resource pool-name="secPool"
                   jndi-name="jdbc/secDS"/>
    <jdbc-connection-pool name="secPool"
                          res-type="javax.sql.DataSource">
        <property name="user" value="root"/>
        <property name="password" value="root"/>
        <property name="url" value="jdbc:mysql://localhost:3306/sec"/>
    </jdbc-connection-pool>
</resources>
```

As you can see, we've just created a data source with the JNDI name `secPool`, and provided it with the required JDBC access information.

Now, the important part here is to tell the new security API that we need to map our users, passwords, and groups to our application by using the `@DatabaseIdentityStoreDefinition` annotation, as follows:

```java
@WebServlet("/home")
@ServletSecurity(@HttpConstraint(rolesAllowed = "user"))
@DatabaseIdentityStoreDefinition(
        dataSourceLookup = "jdbc/secDS",
        callerQuery = "select password from users where username = ?",
        groupsQuery = "select ugroup from users where username = ?"
)
public class HomeServlet extends HttpServlet {
    ...
}
```

Let's see what information we've just told the new security API:

- `dataSourceLookup`: We tell which data source to use for retrieving user information.

- `callerQuery`: The SQL query used to retrieve a password for a specific user. As you can see, we've used a standard SQL `SELECT` statement to retrieve the password in the row where the username is equal to the given one. Note the question mark `?` used in the query: it's a variable parameter that will be obtained from the user input (remember the last screenshot?).
- `groupsQuery`: Like `callerQuery`, this is a SQL query with a parameter. But this time, we've selected `ugroup` rather than the password. This query is responsible, as it's obviously suggesting, for retrieving the group(s) the user is associated with.

So, how is the new security API going to work? When the user tries to access a protected resource, the default HTTP authentication mechanism will be used, displaying a built-in browser authentication dialog where the user shall enter their username and password. After that, the security API implementation will be going to execute `callerQuery` to retrieve the existing user password for the name the user is claiming to be their own. This is the authentication part of the process.

If the password matches the user input one, it will execute the second query, `groupsQuery`. `groupsQuery` will retrieve the group(s) associated with the user. If one of the groups the user belongs to, matches the roles we already specified in the previous step, then they should log in successfully and get the original resource successfully.

Now, run the example again. In the browser authentication dialog, write Tom and tomtom as the username and password, respectively. You should have access without problem, with the original output as follows:

```
Welcome to your home!
```

And, here we go! We've just successfully created our first login example using the new security API, with users and passwords stored on a database.

Identity stores

As mentioned earlier, an identity store is an object that provides access to user's information. An identity store itself is an abstract concept, and there exists many different types of built-in implementations to this abstract concept. And, moreover, you can even define your own custom identity store objects.

In the following sections, we're going to take a closer look at the following types of identity stores:

- Database identity store
- LDAP identity store
- Custom identity store

Database identity store

As shown earlier, a database identity store is used to retrieve user information from a relation database. We've used @DatabaseIdentityStoreDefintion in the first example of this chapter, and here we're going to explore more attributes to this annotation, as shown in this example:

```
@WebServlet("/home")
@ServletSecurity(@HttpConstraint(rolesAllowed = "user"))
@DatabaseIdentityStoreDefinition(
        dataSourceLookup = "jdbc/secDS",
        callerQuery = "select password from users where username = ?",
        groupsQuery = "select ugroup from users where username = ?",
        hashAlgorithm = Pbkdf2PasswordHash.class,
        priority = 10
)
public class HomeServlet extends HttpServlet {
    ...
}
```

LDAP identity store

LDAP is probably the most common way of organizing a user's access to different systems across a single organization. LDAP realizes the idea of Single-Sign On, where a user has a single username and password, and then uses it across all different systems used to perform the everyday business of a specific organization.

Therefore, we naturally find built-in support for the LDAP identity store in the new security API. Although a full LDAP deployment scenario is out of the scope of this book, let's have a quick look at what it looks like to configure a connection with an LDAP server:

```
@WebServlet("/home")
@ServletSecurity(@HttpConstraint(rolesAllowed = "user"))
@LdapIdentityStoreDefinition(
    url = "ldap://localhost:33389/",
    callerBaseDn = "ou=user,dc=jsr375,dc=net",
    groupSearchBase = "ou=group,dc=jsr375,dc=net"
)
public class HomeServlet extends HttpServlet {
    ...
}
```

As you can see, we've used the `@LdapIdentityStore` annotation, passing the following information:

- URL: The URL of the **LDAP** (**Lightweight Directory Access Protocol**) server to use for authentication
- `callerBaseDn`: The base distinguished name for callers (users) in the LDAP store
- `groupSearchBase`: The search base for looking up groups (roles)

Custom identity store

In addition to the built-in identity stores found in the new security API, we can also implement our own identity store, where we can control exactly where we would go to obtain user information.

To do this, we'll need to do the following:

1. Create a custom identity store class.
2. Create an HTTP authentication mechanism associated with this identity store.

Creating a custom identity store class

In this step, we're going to create our custom identity store object, by creating a class that implements the `IdentityStore` interface, as shown in the following example:

```
@ApplicationScoped
public class MyIdentityStore implements IdentityStore {
```

```
        public CredentialValidationResult
   validate(UsernamePasswordCredential userCredential) {
           if (userCredential.compareTo("Tom", "tomtom")) {
               return new CredentialValidationResult("admin",
                       new HashSet<String>(asList("user")));
           }
           return CredentialValidationResult.INVALID_RESULT;
       }
   }
```

In this class, we override the `validate(..)` method of the `IdentityStore` interface. This method is passed a `UsernamePasswordCredential` object, which, as its name suggests, represents a composite of information of the user's claimed username and password.

After that, we've used the `compareTo(...)` method. This method is used to compare the given user/password with the couple of strings we passed to it, respectively. In our example, and for the sake of simplicity, we've just compared it to a hardcoded user/password pair. This is absolutely not applicable in a real-world application, where we should be actually retrieving dynamic (or even fixed) user information from some sort of persistence storage.

Creating an HTTP authentication mechanism

In this step, we'll be creating an HTTP authentication mechanism, which will be used with the identity store class created in the previous step:

```
@ApplicationScoped
public class MyAuthMechanism  implements HttpAuthenticationMechanism {
    @Inject
    private IdentityStoreHandler idStoreHandler;
  public AuthenticationStatus validateRequest(HttpServletRequest req,
                                              HttpServletResponse res,
                                              HttpMessageContext context)
{
        CredentialValidationResult result = idStoreHandler.validate(
               new UsernamePasswordCredential(
                       req.getParameter("name"),
                       req.getParameter("password")));
        if (result.getStatus() == VALID) {
            return context.notifyContainerAboutLogin(result);
        } else {
            return context.responseUnauthorized();
        }
    }
}
```

Our authentication mechanism class implements the `HttpAuthenticationMechanism` superclass, which was introduced in the security API. We override the `validateRequest(...)` method. This method is used to check whether this request is valid to be handled for this user or not. This is typically performed by checking the HTTP request method, alongside the provided user information.

We've used the CDI's `@Inject` annotation to inject an `@IdentityStoreHandler`. This object will be mapped to `IdentityStore`, which we just created in the previous step. In the `validateRequest(...)` method, we've used the identity store's handler `validate(...)` method to check whether the user-provided login information is correct or not. We've encapsulated the user input in a `UsernamePasswordCredential` object, where we've passed a user's given name and password to its constructor.

The returned object, which will be of type `CredentialVaidationResult`, will contain the result of the user validation against the given data. We've checked the status of the result using the `getStatus()` method, and if it has returned the `VALID` constant, this means the user-provided information is correct. In this case, we've returned a notification.

Security context

The security context object is used to programmatically check a user's authority to access a specific resource. This is very useful when you need to do some custom behavior upon having an invalid request from the user, rather than the default one specified by the security API.

In the following example, we're going to forward the user to another page if, and only if, they have access to this page:

```
@WebServlet("/home")
public class HomeServlet extends HttpServlet {

    @Inject
    private SecurityContext securityContext;

    @Override
    protected void doGet(HttpServletRequest req,
HttpServletResponse
    resp)
            throws ServletException, IOException {
    if (securityContext.hasAccessToWebResource("/anotherServlet",
    "GET")) {
        req.getRequestDispatcher("/anotherServlet").forward(req,
```

```
                     res);
                 } else {
                     req.getRequestDispatcher("/logout").forward(req, res);
                 }
             }
         }
```

As you can see, we have used the CDI's `@Inject` annotation to obtain an instance of the security context object. After that, we've used the `hasAccessToWebResource(..)` method to check whether the user has access to the specified resource or not. We've passed two parameters to this method:

- Resource: The URL of the resource we need to check user access against.
- Methods: A `var-args` array representing which HTTP methods we check a user's authority to use. We've only passed `GET` in our example.

Our servlet is going to programmatically check a user's authority on the mentioned resource; if they have the privilege to do so, they will be directed to this resource. Otherwise, we're going to forward them to the login page.

Authentication mechanisms

As mentioned earlier, an authentication mechanism is the way the user identifies themselves to your application via the web browser. In the following sections, we're going to take a closer look at basic and form authentication methods.

Basic authentication

As mentioned earlier, basic authentication displays the browser's native login dialog before the user can access the protected resource. Although this method is not popular in real-world applications now, it's still useful in cases where you need a handy login mechanism for a quick or internal application.

In the following example, we're creating a basic authentication mechanism using the Java new security API:

```
@BasicAuthenticationMechanismDefinition(realmName="user-realm")
@WebServlet("/home")
@DeclareRoles({"user"})
@ServletSecurity(@HttpConstraint(rolesAllowed = "user"))
public class HomeServlet extends HttpServlet {
```

```
    . . .
}
```

Let's see how we annotated our class:

- `@BasicAuthenticationMechanismDefinition`: This annotation obviously declares a basic authentication mechanism for our application. In it, `realmName` represents the one that will be returned in case of login failure, as a value to the WWW-Authenticate header. If you have previous experience with legacy security APIs, don't get confused with Java EE reals, as they are belonging to a completely different realm concepts.
- `@DeclareRoles({"user"})`: This is used to define which roles are supported by the servlet.
- `@ServletSecurity(@HttpConstraint(rolesAllowed = "user"))`: This is used to identify which roles are allowed to access the servlet.

Form authentication

In form authentication, you should be replacing basic HTTP authentication, which is built into the web browser, with your own custom HTML form. For example, you might do the following:

```
<form action="/login">
    <span>Username:</span>
    <input type="text" name="username"/>
    <br/>
    <span>Password:</span>
    <input type="password" name="password"/>
    <br/>
    <button type="submit">Login</button>
</form>
```

Then, we'll create an application `config` class with the `@FormAuthenticationMechanismDefinition` annotation as follows:

```
@FormAuthenticationMechanismDefinition(
    loginToContinue = @LoginToContinue(
            loginPage = "/login",
            errorPage = "/error"
            )
)
@ApplicationScoped
public class ApplicationConfig {
```

```
        . . .
}
```

Let's see what attributes are used in this class:

- @FormAuthenticationMechanismDefinition: Provokes form-based authentication as defined by the servlet 4.0 specification
- loginToContinue: You need to specify login information for this authentication mechanism
- @LoginToContinue: This annotation is used to specify which page should be redirected to if authentication is required, and which page should be redirected to in case of an error

Summary

In this chapter, we have learned about the fundamentals of the new security API, and how we can use it to secure our enterprise applications.

In the next chapter, we're going to learn how to make interactive web apps using the WebSockets API.

Making Interactive Applications with WebSockets 1.1

10

Over recent years, user expectations regarding a more interactive experience with their favorite web applications have greatly increased—more so than desktop applications actually provide. As you may have noticed, desktop products such as the MSN and Yahoo messengers have been replaced with smarter and trendier web application alternatives. The thanks for that go to the World Wide Web Consortium, as their advancements in web technologies have enabled the launch of such amazing products.

Without a doubt, WebSockets is one of the major overall advancements in HTTP communication. It extends HTTP to allow it to handle one or more full-duplex communication channels over a single HTTP connection, enabling all kinds of applications with real-time communication requirements to appear in the web market, such as chatting, multi-player gaming, collaborative document editing, and much more. Therefore, Java naturally includes its own Java WebSockets API, which supports the implementation of WebSockets-powered applications.

In the following sections, we will learn about the following:

- What are WebSockets and when to use it?
- Creating WebSockets endpoints in Java
- Creating WebSockets clients in JavaScript
- Maintaining and encoding user state
- Creating a complete solution using WebSockets

Understanding WebSockets

In the early years of the web, the classic request-response model of HTTP communication put a bottleneck limitation on any application that required the server to send updates directly to the client. To overcome this limitation, the WebSockets protocol was invented.

WebSockets is a TCP protocol that was invented to allow web browsers to open interactive communication sessions with web servers. Unlike HTTP, WebSockets is not based on the request-response communication model. Instead, it opens a full-duplex communication channel with the server, allowing both server and client to exchange messages in real time. This makes it easier to build more creative web apps such as chat, online gaming, real-time statistics, and much more.

Although WebSockets is totally different from HTTP, it's designed specifically to work over the HTTP protocol. Clients perform web-socket connections by handshaking a web server using the HTTP upgrade header, which is the topic of the following section.

How does WebSockets work?

Let's see how the WebSockets protocol works over HTTP. For a client to establish a connection to a web server using WebSockets, it first performs a WebSocket handshake request, which is very similar to a normal HTTP request, but with the Upgrade header, as follows:

```
GET /path/to/endpoint HTTP/1.1
Host: localhost
Upgrade: websocket
Connection: Upgrade
Sec-WebSocket-Key: xqBt3ImNzJbYqRINxEFlkg==
Origin: http://localhost
Sec-WebSocket-Version: 13
```

As you can see, the upgrade header, with some other WebSockets-related headers, is used to perform what's called a WebSockets handshake. The handshake request asks the server to use the WebSockets protocol.

If the web server supports the WebSockets protocol on this path, it should respond with the following handshake response:

```
HTTP/1.1 101 Switching Protocols
Upgrade: websocket
Connection: Upgrade
Sec-WebSocket-Accept: K7DJLdLooIwIG/MOpvWFB3y3FE8=
```

The connection switches to a bi-directional type, and the connection lasts and continues to serve more content, unlike in HTTP, where the connection is closed instantaneously.

Sending and receiving messages

In the following example, we will look at how to send and receive messages using WebSockets technology. We will use a Java WebSocket endpoint as the backend for this example, and HTML and JavaScript as the frontend, to see how can we communicate within our typical web page.

Creating an endpoint

Let's start with the backend part of the example.

A WebSockets application consists of a set of endpoints, each endpoint providing a communication channel that clients can connect to. In the Java WebSockets API, endpoints can be created easily using annotations. Just annotate your class with `@ServerEndpoint` to be able to serve WebSockets connections, as shown in the following example:

```
@ServerEndpoint("/echo")
public class EchoEndpoint {
....
}
```

The `EchoEndpoint` class now is a WebSocket endpoint resource that is able to accept client connections and perform two-way communication with them. The string parameter `"/echo"` represents the URL that this endpoint is mapped to.

Now, let's design a WebSocket endpoint, which will accept client connections, read any received messages, and respond with the same sent message preceded by a prefix.

Create a class, `EchoEndpoint`, with the following code:

```
@ServerEndpoint("/echo")
public class EchoEndpoint {

    @OnMessage
    public void onMessage(Session session, String msg) {
        System.out.println("Message received: " + msg);

        try {
            // send a message (response) to the remote peer
            String response = "You sent: " + msg;
            session.getBasicRemote().sendText(response);
        } catch (IOException ex) {
            ex.printStackTrace();
        }

    }

}
```

In the preceding code, we used `@ServerEndpoint` to declare our class as a WebSocket endpoint. The `"/echo"` parameter represents the URL that will be used to connect to it.

Note that the server endpoint's URL is relative to your web application's context path.

We have declared the `onMessage(Session, String)` method, annotated with the `@OnMessage` annotation. As ought to be clear, this method will be called whenever a new message is delivered from a connected client. `@OnMessage` is a lifecycle annotation that tells the Java WebSockets API that the annotated method is meant to be fired upon new messages. The two passed parameters are as follows:

- Session session: An instance of type `Session`, which represents an open communication session with a remote client. This object is used to send messages back to the client, maintain user states, iterate through other open sessions, and much more.
- String message: The message delivered by the client.

In the following section, we will look at how to connect to this web socket and send some messages to it, but for now, let's examine the implementation of the `onMessage` method. We have used the `session` object to send a message to the client, using `session.getBasicRemote().sendText(String)`. The `session.getBasicRemote()` method returns a reference to the remote peer that is able to send messages to it. The `sendText(String)` method, as the name suggests, is used to send a text message to the remote client.

Creating a client web page

In this section, we will create an HTML page with the following content:

As you can see, on this page we have the following:

- An input
- A **Send** button
- A **Log** area

Once the page loads, we will connect to the endpoint with JavaScript. Once a connection is established successfully, a `Connection opened` message should be displayed in the log area. When the user writes some data in the input, then clicks **Send**, the message should be sent to the server, which will respond by echoing the message, prefixed by `RECEIVED:`. Each message sent or received should be logged in the log area, as shown in the previous screenshot.

Let's create an `index.html` file with the following code, to get the content shown in the screenshot:

```html
<!DOCTYPE html>
<html>
  <head>...</head>
  <body>
    <h1>Message Sender</h1>
    <input id="message"/> <!-- (1) the input -->
    <button onclick="send()">Send</button> <!-- (2) the send button -->
      <h2>Log</h2>
      <div id="log_container"></div> <!-- (3) logs area -->
      <script>
          // script goes here
      </script>
  </body>
</html>
```

Note that, if you are not familiar with HTML and JS, you can continue to use the code for testing purposes without needing to understand every single line of code in the previous and following code snippets.

Now, in the script area, let's write some JavaScript to connect to the backend:

```javascript
// create a websocket connection object with the remote endpoint
var ws = new WebSocket("ws://localhost:9354/ch10_websockets/echo");
```

This will create a `websocket` object, which will connect to the URL passed to the JS object's constructor. Like in Java WebSockets, JS WebSockets introduce lifecycle events, which we can attach our handler to as follows:

```javascript
// fired when the connection opens
ws.onopen = function () {
    log("Connection opened");
};
```

Now, when the connection is established successfully, the previously declared function will be executed. We will log a message denoting that a connection has been opened using a custom `log` function (this will be shown in a later section).

Then, it's time to handle user click event on send button:

```
// fired on click on send button
// sends a message user written in the input to the remote endpoint
function send() {
    // retrieve input value
    var msg = document.getElementById("message").value;
    // send the message
    ws.send(msg);
    log("SENT: " + msg);
    document.getElementById("message").value = "";
}
```

This function is used in the HTML as the click handler for the send button. As you see, upon clicking the **Send** button, we retrieve the value for the input to use as our message, use WebSockets' `send` function to send the message, then empty the input again.

Then, in order to handle the server response to this message, we shall attach a handler to the `onMessage` event of the `websocket` object, as follows:

```
// fired when the server sends a message
ws.onmessage = function (evt) {
    log("RECEIEVED: " + evt.data);
};
```

Upon receiving a message, this function will be executed. We will log the message, which is stored in the event's object data attribute.

Now, to complete the example, let's declare the `log` function:

```
// used to log an event
// display each log in a new line
function log(text) {
    var newP = document.createElement("p");
    newP.innerHTML = text;
    document.getElementById("log_container").appendChild(newP);
}
```

As you can see, the `log` function takes a `text` parameter, then creates a new paragraph element containing the passed text, then appends this as a child of this document.

Now, you can run the example and try it yourself!

Lifecycle events

As shown previously, the `@OnMessage` lifecycle method is used to handle the primary communication event, which is the delivery of a new message. Other lifecycle events are often used to handle other events of interest. The following table shows the four lifecycle events that are triggered by the WebSockets endpoint:

Annotation	Event	Example

@OnOpen	Connection opened	`@OnOpen`
		`public void open(Session session,`
		`EndpointConfig conf) { }`

@OnClose	Connection closed	`@OnClose`
		`public void close(Session session,`
		`CloseReason reason) { }`

@OnMessage	Message arrived	`@OnMessage`
		`public void message(Session session,`
		`String msg) { }`

@OnError	Connection error	`@OnError`
		`public void error(Session session,`
		`Throwable error) { }`

Accepting path parameters

Just as in RESTful services, we can accept path parameters through the URL to which the client tries to connect. Path parameters are useful in case you have multiple contexts of the same service, for example, a chatroom service.

To use path parameters, write a `{PARAM_NAME}` expression in the URL pattern, as follows:

```
@ServerEndpoint("/rooms/{roomName}/{username}")
public class RoomsEndpoint {

    @OnOpen
    public void onOpen(Session session, EndpointConfig endpointConfig,
            @PathParam("roomName") String roomName,
            @PathParam("username") String username) {
        System.out.println("room " + roomName);
        System.out.println("user " + username);
    }
}
```

As you can see, we have included `{roomName}` and `{username}` as two path parameters that should be passed by the user. To connect to this endpoint, you need to use a URL such as the following:

```
Example URL > ws://localhost:9354/ch10_websockets/rooms/room1/user1
```

The values of `roomName` and `username` will be mapped to `room1` and `user1`, respectively. You can obtain those parameters in any WebSocket lifecycle event method, by introducing parameters annotated with `@PathParam`, like in RESTful services.

Maintaining user state

It's very likely that you may want to store some user state associated with each session. In this case, you can safely use instance variables to maintain this state, as each connection creates a unique instance of the `endpoint` class.

Moreover, there is an extra associated map with the `session` object, where you can store and retrieve user state. Although instance variables will do, the `session` object is useful in cases where you need to expose those states to other sessions of the same endpoint. In situations such as chatting, you may loop over all open sessions and examine each session's username, to check whether this message should be delivered to them or not.

Let's look at how can we use this extra map in practice. Suppose we are designing a WebSockets endpoint for a chat room; we will accept connections on `/rooms/{roomName}/{username}`. For each new user joining a room, we will send him/her the names of all the users in this room (including themselves). We will extend the example shown in the previous section, as follows:

```java
@ServerEndpoint("/rooms/{roomName}/{username}")
public class RoomsEndpoint {

    @OnOpen
    public void onOpen(Session session, EndpointConfig endpointConfig,
            @PathParam("roomName") String roomName,
            @PathParam("username") String username) {

        // set room name and username in the properties map
        session.getUserProperties().put("roomName", roomName);
        session.getUserProperties().put("username", username);

        // send all other user names in the same room to this user
        for (Session openSession : session.getOpenSessions()) {
            String room = (String)
```

```
openSession.getUserProperties().get("roomName");
            // if user in the same room
            if (room.equals(roomName)) {
                String user = (String)
openSession.getUserProperties().get("username");
                try {
                    // send the username to this user
                    session.getBasicRemote().sendText(user);
                } catch (IOException ex) {
                    ex.printStackTrace();
                }
            }
        }
    }
}
```

After storing `roomName` and `username` as states for the current user, we have fetched all open sessions using the `session.getOpenSession()` method, looped over all sessions, and checked whether the session belongs to the same room, to send the username of this session to the current user. You can write your own JS code to test this.

Using encoders

In the previous examples, we exchanged messages only of type `string`. Sometimes, we may need to transfer more complex objects to the client, a `Movie` instance, for example, holding information such as the movie title, actors, and so on. From a RESTful background, the most popular solution is to convert the object to a JSON string. Rather than doing this manually before using the `sendText(String)` method, we can define a custom encode that automatically converts the object to the desired format.

Let's look at the following example:

```
@ServerEndpoint(value = "/movie/{movieId}",
        encoders = {MovieEncoder.class})
public class MoviesEndpoint{
    public void onOpen(Session session, EndpointConfig endpointConfig)
{
        Movie movie = new Movie();
        try {
            // fill with some data
            session.getBasicRemote().sendObject(movie);
        } catch (IOException | EncodeException ex) {
            ex.printStackTrace();
```

```
                    }
                }
            }
```

In this example, we have used the sendObject(Object) method rather than the sendText(String) method. In order for this method to work properly, we have declared an encoder using the encoders property of the @ServerEndpoint annotation. We have assigned a value of MovieEncoder.class, which is a custom encoder class we will show in the following lines.

To create an encoder, create a class that implements the Encoder.Text<T> interface, passing the T type of the type you are converting to, which is Movie in our case, as follows:

```
public class MovieEncoder implements Encoder.Text<Movie> {

    @Override
    public String encode(Movie movie) throws EncodeException {
        Jsonb jsonb = JsonbBuilder.create();
        return jsonb.toJson(jsonb);
    }

    @Override
    public void init(EndpointConfig endpointConfig) {}

    @Override
    public void destroy() {}
}
```

The interface includes four methods to implement:

- init: Implement to perform any resource allocation or initial actions
- destroy: Implement to perform any resource releasing or final actions
- encode: This is the important one; its implementation should actually perform conversion between the given type (Movie in our example) and string

As you can see, in our implementation to the encode method, we have used Jsonb (previously discussed in Chapter 7, *Manipulating JSON with JSON-B 1.0*), to convert the movie object to a string value.

Seat-booking application

In the following sections, we will create a more advanced application to put together everything we have learned in this chapter.

In a cinema booking application, you typically get prompted with a diagram of available seats, where you can choose one or more seats to book. One of the primary features of such an application is to keep the user updated with any new bookings that have been made while he is still choosing his favorite seats. We will implement a scenario where the user can choose one or more seats, without choosing some other seats being booked in the same moment.

Our application should look as follows:

Book a Seat

Seats for Movie with ID 27

001	002	003	004	005	006	007	008	009	010	011	012
013	014	015	016	017	018	019	020	021	022	023	024
025	026	027	028	029	030	031	032	033	034	035	036
037	038	039	040	041	042	043	044	045	046	047	048
049	050	051	052	053	054	055	056	057	058	059	060
061	062	063	064	065	066	067	068	069	070	071	072
073	074	075	076	077	078	079	080	081	082	083	084
085	086	087	088	089	090	091	092	093	094	095	096
097	098	099	100	101	102	103	104	105	106	107	108
109	110	111	112	113	114	115	116	117	118	119	120
121	122	123	124	125	126	127	128	129	130	131	132
133	134	135	136	137	138	139	140	141	142	143	144
145	146	147	148	149	150	151	152	153	154	155	156
157	158	159	160	161	162	163	164	165	166	167	168

As you can see, the page shows a simple seat matrix to the user as HTML buttons arranged in a grid. The text color for buttons is as follows:

- Black: Available seats
- Red: Seats booked by other users
- Green: Seats booked by the current user

For the user to book an available seat, all he has to do is click on the seat's button. It should go green (as it has been booked by the current user), while all other users opening the same page for the same movie should instantaneously see those buttons in red.

For the sake of simplicity, we have ignored other details such as movies and date choices; the user will simply access this page using the following URL:
`http://localhost:9354/ch10_websockets/ex3.html?movieId=27`

We will manually write an arbitrary number for the movie ID as a path parameter. Our backend will initialize data for the specified ID on the first request.

Designing and implementing the backend

For the backend, we will use a WebSocket endpoint mapped to the URL `/booking/{movieId}`, as follows:

```
@ServerEndpoint(value = "/booking/{movieId}",
                         encoders = {SeatsEncoder.class})
public class BookingEndpoint {
    ...
}
```

Inside the endpoint class, we will define an in-memory database to simulate a database for all available movies. In a real-world implementation, the database would be too complex to maintain movies, available dates and cinemas, and seats for each combination in persistent storage. However, for the sake of simplicity, we will create a `HashMap` of `Integer` to `boolean[][]`, where the key will be the movie ID, and the value a two-dimensional array of Boolean values, denoting whether the seat is booked or not. We are completely ignoring date and cinema details.

Let's introduce our `HashMap` as follows:

```
// in-memory database for movies booking state
private static final HashMap<Integer, boolean[][]> seatsDatabase = new HashMap<>();
```

When a new session is created, we will do the following actions:

1. Associate the user properties map for this session with the `movieId` the user requires to book in
2. Send the user the current state of the available seats

To do this, we will write the following method in our endpoint class:

```
@OnOpen
public void open(Session session, EndpointConfig conf,
@PathParam("movieId") int movieId) {
    try {
        // remember which movieId this session is connected to
        session.getUserProperties().put("movieId", movieId);
        // send initial booking matrix state for this movie
        boolean[][] movieSeats = getMovieSeats(movieId);
        session.getBasicRemote().sendObject(movieSeats);
    } catch (EncodeException | IOException ex) {
        ex.printStackTrace();
    }
}
```

In the preceding lines of code, we first stored the `movieId` in the user properties map; this will be used later in another scenario. After that, we obtained the movie seats' state using the `getMovieSeats(int)` method, the implementation of which we will explain in the following section. This method will simply look up the map for a key with this movie ID, and if it does not exist (on the first request), create, store, and retrieve a new state (with all values initialized to false, denoting that all seats are available to book). Then, this state is sent to the new client using the `sendObject(Object)` method. An appropriate encoder should be used to convert this `boolean[][]` value to text, which will be shown later.

Now, let's have a look at the `getMovieSeats` method. Note that when creating a seat state for a movie for the first time, we consider that any cinema has seats arranged in a grid of 14 rows and 12 columns:

```
// retrieve the booking matrix for a specific movie
private boolean[][] getMovieSeats(int movieId) {
    // get the booking matrix for this movie
    boolean[][] movieSeats = seatsDatabase.get(movieId);
    // if it does not exist, create a newone
    if (movieSeats == null) {
        movieSeats = new boolean[14][12];
        seatsDatabase.put(movieId, movieSeats);
    }
    // return the booking matrix
    return movieSeats;
}
```

Now, let's implement the most critical feature of this application—booking a seat. We will design our endpoint such that it receives a message in the format book {seatId}, where seatId is a serial number for a cinema seat. If, for example, the user requested to book the 17th seat, it would be the fifth column in the second row (remember, we are in a matrix of 14 x 12).

So, we will implement the onMessage lifecycle event so that it parses the seat index, calculates its corresponding row and column, and sets the value in this position of the seat matrix for the movie to be true (the booked flag).

After that, we will do a more advanced job. We will notify all customers currently joining the booking process for this movie that this movie is fully booked and no longer available for booking. We will do this by looping over all open sessions and checking for the associated state of movieId. If this session has the same movie ID, then a notification will be sent to the peer associated with this session in the following format: booked {seatId}. The frontend will later process this message and perform the appropriate action.

Let's examine the code for this:

```
@OnMessage
public void onMessage(Session session, String msg,
@PathParam("movieId") int movieId) {
    // Retrieve the booking matrix for this movie
    boolean[][] movieSeats = getMovieSeats(movieId);

    if (msg.startsWith("book ")) {
        // a booking request from this user
        // extract seat index
        int seatIndex = Integer.parseInt(msg.substring(5));

        // identify its row and column in the booking matrix
        int row = seatIndex / movieSeats[0].length;
        int col = seatIndex % movieSeats[0].length;
        // set the status of this seat to be booked
        movieSeats[row][col] = true;

        // notify all users connected to this movie session
        // that this book has been booked
        for (Session openSession : session.getOpenSessions()) {
            if ((Integer)
openSession.getUserProperties().get("movieId") != movieId) {
                continue;
            }
            try {
                openSession.getBasicRemote().sendText("booked " +
```

```
seatIndex);
                } catch (IOException ex) {
                    ex.printStackTrace();
                }
            }
        }
    }
}
```

Remember the encoder? In this example, I will use a simple zero, one, pipe encoding pattern for the seats state. For example, 0010 | 0000 | 0000 would mean we have four columns and three rows with matrix[0][2] set to true, and all other values set to false.

Let's examine the code for this:

```java
public class SeatsEncoder implements Encoder.Text<boolean[][]> {

    @Override
    public String encode(boolean[][] seats) throws EncodeException {
        StringBuilder sb = new StringBuilder();
        sb.append("seats ");
        for (int i = 0; i < seats.length; i++) {
            for (int j = 0; j < seats[i].length; j++) {
                sb.append(seats[i][j] ? "1" : "0");
            }
            if (i != seats.length - 1) {
                sb.append("|");
            }
        }

        return sb.toString();

    }

    @Override
    public void init(EndpointConfig config) {}

    @Override
    public void destroy() {}

}
```

Note that I've added a prefix of seats to the encoded text so that the message can be identified by the client side, as will be shown in the frontend section.

Designing and implementing the frontend

Let's go further by implementing the frontend of our application. Create an `index.html` file with the following content:

```html
<!DOCTYPE html>
<html>
    <head>
        <style>
            button:disabled { color: red; }
            .my-booking:disabled { font-weight: bold; color: green; }
        </style>
    </head>
    <body>
        <h1>Book a Seat</h1>
        <h2 id="movie-label">Seats</h2> <!-- wraps movie id -->
        <div id="seats_container"/>  <!-- wraps seats buttons matrix -->

        <script>
            // script goes here
        </script>
    </body>
</html>
```

In our HTML, we have included two key UI elements:

- `movie-label`: A label that displays the current movie ID
- `seats_container`: A div that will contain the buttons matrix for the current movie seats

Now, let's write the required script. We request this page with the following URL: `http://localhost:9354/ch10_websockets/ex3.html?movieId=27`.

We will read this movie ID and show it in the movie label with the following code:

```javascript
var url = window.location.href;
var movieId = url.substring(url.indexOf("movieId=") + 8);

document.getElementById("movie-label").innerHTML = "Seats for Movie
with ID " + movieId;
```

Then, we will perform a connection with the backend's endpoint, passing the `movieId` as a path `param`, as follows:

```
// connects to booking channel for this movie
var ws = new WebSocket("ws://localhost:9354/ch10_websockets/booking/" +
movieId);
```

According to our backend design, the client may receive two types of message:

1. Messages start with seats, which includes the initial seat state for the current movie
2. Messages start with the book, which provides details of seats already booked, including those booked by the current user

We will implement the JS WebSocket's `onmessage` as follows:

1. Fetch message
2. If it starts with available seats, extract seat code, then decode and render the corresponding buttons
3. If it starts with booked seats, extract `seatId`, then update the corresponding button to match the new state

Let's examine the code for this:

```
ws.onmessage = function (evt) {
    var msg = evt.data;
    if (msg.startsWith("seats ")) {
        // initial message with seats status
        msg = msg.substring(6);
        buildSeats(msg);
    } else if (msg.startsWith("booked ")) {
        // a new booking has been performed
        // by the current or another user
        msg = msg.substring(7);
        var seatId = parseInt(msg);
        buttons[seatId].disabled = true;
    }
};
```

In the first case, we called the `buildSeats` function. We will look at this function in further detail soon, as it may seem a bit complex if you are unfamiliar with JavaScript. What it does, simply, is to read the encoded representation of seats, split and parse them, then create and build buttons to the `seats_container` div. The button will be disabled if the corresponding Boolean value is set to `true`, and vice versa. This function will be called once per visit, and all created buttons will be pushed to a buttons array as follows:

```
var buttons = [];
function buildSeats(seatsCode) {
    var seatsContainer = document.getElementById("seats_container");

    var rows = seatsCode.split("|");
    var counter = 0;
    for (var i = 0; i < rows.length; i++) {
        var rowCode = rows[i];
        for (var j = 0; j < rowCode.length; j++) {
            var booked = rowCode.substring(j, j + 1) === "1" ? true :
false;

            var button = document.createElement("button");
            buttons.push(button);
            counter++;
            var label = "" + counter;
            if (counter < 10) {
                label = "00" + label;
            } else if (counter < 100) {
                label = "0" + label;
            }
            button.innerHTML = label;
            button.disabled = booked;
            seatsContainer.appendChild(button);

            button.onclick = function () {
                ws.send("book " + (parseInt(this.innerHTML) - 1));
                this.classList.add("my-booking");
            };
        }
        seatsContainer.appendChild(document.createElement("br"));
    }
}
```

The previous code parses the string, loops over rows and columns, creates button elements and sets their disabled state, then appends to the container and the button array. The `onclick` function for each button will send a booking request to the endpoint as shown previously, then append a special CSS class to the button. This class is responsible for setting the button to green rather than red, when later notified about getting booked by you! It's a bit of a dummy workaround, to simplify this example without worrying about any other useful details.

Now, back to the `onmessage` case. Let's examine the second case, when the server notifies us that a seat has been booked. We will fetch the seat index, then use the buttons array to refer to the corresponding button and set it to disabled. The CSS trick works as follows: the disabled state for buttons has a red foreground by default. If the button was appended to the CSS class `my-booking`, this will override this property to green. We set this to a button before booking it; therefore, it will turn green for you, and red for the others! This is not safe to use in a real-world scenario with concurrent usage, but again, this is for the sake of simplicity for this application.

Now you can run the application and try it yourself. In order to test the green/red scenario, you should use multiple browser tabs for the same URL for a specific `movieId`. Each tab will be considered a separate user for the endpoint.

Summary

In this chapter, we have learned how to write a WebSockets endpoint in Java, and how to communicate with it using a JavaScript frontend. We have built a real-world application using WebSockets, to handle the conflicts of a group of users reserving seats in a cinema at the same time, where we have seen the important role WebSockets had to play.

Well, we have finally reached the end of our book, and I can't tell you what we are going to learn in the next chapter, as there are no more chapters! However, there is still plenty that you can learn about Java EE, and I hope this book has increased your appetite for it!

Other Books You May Enjoy

If you enjoyed this book, you may be interested in these other books by Packt:

Java EE 8 Cookbook
Elder Moraes

ISBN: 9781788293037

- Actionable information on the new features of Java EE 8
- Using the most important APIs with real and working code
- Building server side applications, web services, and web applications
- Deploying and managing your application using the most important Java EE servers
- Building and deploying microservices using Java EE 8
- Building Reactive application by joining Java EE APIs and core Java features
- Moving your application to the cloud using containers
- Practical ways to improve your projects and career through community involvement

Java EE 8 High Performance
Romain Manni-Bucau

ISBN: 9781788473064

- Identify performance bottlenecks in an application
- Locate application hotspots using performance tools
- Understand the work done under the hood by EE containers and its impact on performance
- Identify common patterns to integrate with Java EE applications
- Implement transparent caching on your applications
- Extract more information from your applications using Java EE without modifying existing code
- Ensure constant performance and eliminate regression

Leave a review - let other readers know what you think

Please share your thoughts on this book with others by leaving a review on the site that you bought it from. If you purchased the book from Amazon, please leave us an honest review on this book's Amazon page. This is vital so that other potential readers can see and use your unbiased opinion to make purchasing decisions, we can understand what our customers think about our products, and our authors can see your feedback on the title that they have worked with Packt to create. It will only take a few minutes of your time, but is valuable to other potential customers, our authors, and Packt. Thank you!

Index